OSPREY AIRCRAFT OF THE ACES • 100

Ki-44 'Tojo' Aces of World War 2

SERIES EDITOR: TONY HOLMES

OSPREY AIRCRAFT OF THE ACES • 100

Ki-44 'Tojo' Aces of World War 2

Nicholas Millman

OSPREY
PUBLISHING

Front Cover
Flying a black-painted Ki-44, 1Lt Hideaki Inayama of the 87th Sentai attacks a Fleet Air Arm Avenger II during Operation *Meridian*, which saw aircraft from the Royal Navy's Pacific Fleet strike the oil refineries at Sungai Gerong and Plaju, in Sumatra, on 24 January 1945. After engagements with the first wave of Avengers and Hellcats, 1Lt Inayama described an encounter with two Avengers that he intercepted as they egressed the target area at low level;

'I carefully turned in behind them, concentrating on the damaged Avenger, which still had its bomb doors open – his hydraulics had probably been damaged. Six hundred yards, five hundred yards – suddenly its ball turret gunner opened fire. Red tracers slipped past my Shoki, but I held my fire. Two hundred yards – I could clearly see the gunner in the ball turret. Now I was flying in the wash of my quarry and my aircraft was bouncing around like a mad thing. Steadying the Shoki, I fired at point blank distance. The bullets from my four 13 mm machine guns ripped into the Avenger, its greenhouse canopy bursting into fragments like leaves in a gale. Flames seared back from the port wing root, and the Avenger rolled over onto its back and then fell away into the jungle below.'

Inayama then attempted to attack the second Avenger that appeared to be badly damaged, with a large hole near the starboard wingtip and its ball turret apparently unoccupied. He climbed above it, intending to make a diving attack to finish the aircraft off, but his delay allowed the Avenger pilot to reach cloud cover and escape. The Avenger he attacked first might have been JZ331 from 849 Naval Air Squadron, flown by Sub-Lts H E Stalker RNZNVR and J W R Lynn and PO H Copping. The crew survived the encounter (although Lynn was wounded) and recovered their badly damaged aircraft back aboard the aircraft carrier HMS *Victorious* (Cover artwork by Ronnie Olsthoorn)

Dedication

In memory of all the young men who flew, fought and died for their countries in World War 2

First published in Great Britain in 2011 by Osprey Publishing
Midland House, West Way, Botley, Oxford, OX2 0PH
44-02 23rd Street, Suite 219, Long Island City, NY, 11101, USA

E-mail; info@ospreypublishing.com

Osprey Publishing is part of the Osprey Group

A CIP catalogue record for this book is available from the British Library

ISBN: 978 1 84908 440 6
e-book ISBN: 978 1 84908 441 3

Edited by Tony Holmes
Page design by Tony Truscott
Cover Artwork, Aircraft Profiles and Scale Drawings by Ronnie Olsthoorn
Index by Marie-Pierre Evans
Originated by PDQ Digital Media Solutions
Printed and bound in China through Bookbuilders

11 12 13 14 15   10 9 8 7 6 5 4 3 2 1

Osprey Publishing is supporting the Woodland Trust, the UK's leading woodland conservation charity by funding the dedication of trees.

www.ospreypublishing.com

ACKNOWLEDGEMENTS
The author gratefully acknowledges the kind assistance of the following contributors – *Arawasi*, Graham Boak, Mary-Grace Browning, Richard Dunn, Martin Ferkl, Ken Glass, Mark Haselden, Ryusuke Ishiguro, Dr Yasuho Izawa, C W Lam, James F Lansdale, Jöern Leckscheid, James I Long, Robert Mikesh, Carl Molesworth, Keishiro Nagao, Joe Picarella, Henry Sakaida, Summer, Akio Takahashi and Hiroshi Umemoto.

CONTENTS

INTRODUCTION

The Japanese Army Air Force's Nakajima-built Type 2 heavy fighter, popularly known as the Ki-44 (Ki stands for kitai, meaning airframe type number) Shoki, or by its Allied reporting name 'Tojo', was developed from a Koku Hombu (Air Headquarters) requirement for a heavy fighter that was substantially different in concept to contemporary Japanese fighter aircraft. The design project was assigned to Yasushi Koyama, and it ran almost in parallel with the development of Nakajima's Type 1 single-seat 'light' fighter, the Ki-43 Hayabusa (Peregrine Falcon), Allied reporting name 'Oscar' (see *Osprey Aircraft of the Aces 85 – Ki-43 'Oscar' Aces of World War 2* for the aircraft's service details).

Whereas the JAAF had hitherto placed emphasis on the responsiveness and agility of fighter aircraft to undertake classic dogfighting in World War 1 style, this new machine was to incorporate speed, rate-of-climb and the ability to withstand considerable battle damage in preference to manoeuvrability. Although the Ki-44 is often characterised as an air defence or interceptor fighter, the requirement for the advanced heavy fighter was firmly engrained within a JAAF hierarchy that had already totally embraced the concept of 'aerial exterminating action'. The latter meant the positive and autonomous surveillance and complete

A stripped airframe reveals the skeletal structure of the Ki-44 as maintenance apprentices listen attentively to their instructor at the Tokorozawa Army Maintenance Technical School. The latter held instructional airframes of most aircraft types in JAAF service. The large hatch in the fuselage was primarily to provide access to the radio equipment (*Summer*)

destruction of enemy aircraft in the air and on the ground at their airfields. This concept eschewed the importance of a complementary defensive posture, the offensive doctrine reaching all levels within the JAAF. It was to have a significant impact on the way that this new aircraft would be deployed.

The 1939 specifications for the new fighter were couched loosely, but they required the maximum speed to exceed 372 mph at an altitude of 13,000 ft, a range of 746 miles and the capability to climb to 16,500 ft at normal combat weight in less than five minutes. The development programme was not without its problems, as initial speeds were disappointing and the prototype aircraft was humiliated in trials comparing it with the Imperial Japanese Navy's new Mitsubishi A6M Zero-sen. The latter at first proved to be equal to the Ki-44 in its rate-of-climb and faster in level flight. The design team persisted in its efforts to overcome these shortcomings, however, and with great skill reached a point where the Koku Hombu was both satisfied and ready to commit the pre-production Ki-44 to operational trials in actual combat conditions in China.

The wing loading of the new aircraft was high and landing speeds consequentially fast, which made for tricky handling. Initially, the fighter was envisaged to be flown only by experienced pilots with more than 1000 flying hours in their log books, but later this caution was found to be excessive. Indeed, by the late war period it was determined that even relatively inexperienced pilots who had no preconceptions of flying earlier highly manoeuvrable aircraft such as the Nakajima Ki-27 and Ki-43 could cope with the Ki-44 satisfactorily.

On the plus side, the aircraft became a superb gun platform, its pilots invariably scoring the highest points in gunnery competitions against other JAAF and IJN fighters. The Ki-44 also possessed excellent dive and climb characteristics, which in turn permitted fast hit-and-run tactics to be employed. When these were first introduced by Shoki units in China, they represented a radical departure from the 'traditional' JAAF 'dogfighting' tactics that placed a heavy emphasis on aerobatics, tight turns and extreme manoeuvrability.

Pilot opinion of aircraft capability is often subjective, and such is human nature that opinions can differ widely, even in respect of the same aircraft. Most sources agree that initial concerns over the Ki-44's lack of manoeuvrability and high landing speed, expressed by pilots used to such nimble performers as the Ki-27 and Ki-43, were replaced by respect by those aviators who were able to exploit and enjoy the Shoki's best qualities – 'a rapid roll rate, outstanding dive characteristics and excellence as a gun platform'.

Unsurprisingly, the Ki 44 found its greatest exponents in units that had transitioned to the new aircraft directly from the Ki-27, like the 85th Hiko Sentai (Air Regiment), or who had flown it from the outset, like the 47th Hiko Sentai. Those units flying the Ki-43 who later augmented their air defence capability with small numbers of Ki-44s tended to be unimpressed and disparaging of the new type, being firmly wedded to the concept of manoeuvre combat exemplified by the 'Oscar'. This suspicion about the aircraft's capabilities was reinforced by the fact that only a very small number of pilots were able to become aces flying the

Ki-44. Those who were ready both to accept the aircraft's characteristics and to exploit them fully in combat were few and far between.

This limited success, however, was partly because the Ki-44 was only ever produced in relatively small numbers – a total of 1227 aircraft, representing barely nine percent of JAAF single-engined fighter production in World War 2.

Outside Japan, where the aircraft is most commonly associated with anti-B-29 Home Island defence operations, the Ki-44's most significant deployment was in China, but it was also used in the East Indies, Burma and the Philippines. Curiously, the Shoki was not used at all in the tide-turning maelstrom of the New Guinea theatre. This was probably because the JAAF had already decided that strategic air defence units in Japan, China and the East Indies should receive the new aircraft first. The Ki-44 was also issued in small numbers to those fighter units equipped primarily with other types so as to provide them with an improved bomber interception/air defence capability.

In common with some other JAAF types, the Ki-44 has tended to be underestimated or disregarded by aviation writers. The common reporting soubriquet of 'Zero' for all types of Japanese fighters encountered in China has resulted in a presumption that many combats involved only Ki-43 'Oscars' (usually misidentified by Allied pilots as a 'Zero'). In one recent published account, the Ki-44 was described as being 'cobbled together from a Hayabusa airframe and a 1500 hp bomber engine'. That it certainly was not, and such a description does scant justice to the outstanding efforts of Professor Hideo Itokawa and his design team in successfully meeting the 1939 requirement for a heavy fighter possessing almost revolutionary, but certainly radical, capabilities for the JAAF.

Without special pleading, this book seeks to introduce a wider readership to the existence and exploits of this unusual Japanese fighter, and to some of the aces and notable pilots who flew it in battle.

The Ki-44 was named Shoki for the semi-mythical Taoist temple deity who could destroy or frighten away demons and devils. Shoki was usually depicted, as in this ivory netsuke, as a fierce-faced, bearded man armed with a sword (*Los Angeles County Museum of Art*)

The early morning sun glints on Shokis of the 70th Sentai as mechanics prepare them for flying in the air defence of Japan. In the foreground a Ki-44-Hei fitted with a reflector gunsight, whilst behind it is an earlier Ki-44-II Otsu with a telescopic optical site and without wing armament. The 70th Sentai was a successful Ki-44 unit, using the type until the end of the war and generating a number of notable pilots and aces (*via Robert Mikesh*)

KINGFISHER FORCE

Prior to Japan's attack on the Western Allies in December 1941, its Army Air Headquarters had watched the conflict in Europe with close interest. Secret intelligence reports from the air attachés in Berlin and London included not just assessments of the capabilities of Luftwaffe and RAF aircraft, but also the development of air doctrine over Europe and the influence of combat experience from both sides.

An awareness of an increasing emphasis on altitude, hit-and-run tactics and an expectation that the RAF would deploy the Spitfire to defend their Far Eastern possessions accelerated commitment of the Shoki to Japan's initial attack. Consequently it was decided that the aircraft's pre-production trials would not be confined to China, but would instead become part of the Japanese attack on Malaya. An experimental unit of pre-production Ki-44s would be formed to test the aircraft – and its concept – in battle. Here was the second departure, because the Ki-44 would be committed from the outset to an offensive fighter role, which was somewhat challenging to its design profile.

In August 1941 leadership of the JAAF's experimental unit was assigned to 31-year-old Maj Toshio Sakagawa from Hyogo Prefecture. He had served with the 11th Rentai and 24th Sentai in China, but had had little opportunity to engage in combat. Sakagawa was, however, a dynamic and proficient leader who would later command the Ki-43 'Oscar'-equipped 25th Sentai almost throughout the entire campaign in China, before being killed in the accidental crash of a transport aircraft returning him to Japan from the Philippines on the night of 19 December 1944. He would be credited with approximately 15 victories at the time of his death.

Sakagawa's new experimental unit was formed at Tachikawa airfield, in Japan, in early September 1941. Staffed with experienced personnel assigned from the JAAF's Flight Test Centre, it was designated the Dokuritsu 47th Hiko Chutai (Independent 47th Air Squadron). Its name was said to be in recognition of the legendary Japanese tale of the 47 Ronin, a band of samurai who took revenge for their assassinated leader. However, the unit became unofficially known as the Kawasemi Butai (Kingfisher Force), reflecting the new tactics that were to be pioneered, or rather more informally the Shinsengumi ('newly selected band' or 'chosen ones'). On 5 September seven pre-production aircraft and the second and third Ki-44 prototypes were issued to the new unit as its primary equipment.

The engine chosen for the new fighter was the Nakajima Ha-41 of 1250 hp that had been developed for heavy bombers, and whose powerful bulk was

Maj Toshio Sakagawa led the JAAF's first Ki-44 unit, the 47th Chutai, at the start of the Pacific War. Seen here as commander of the 25th Sentai in China, flying the Ki-43 Hayabusa, Maj Sakagawa claimed a total of 15 victories before being killed in a flying accident on 19 December 1944 (*Yasuho Izawa*)

9

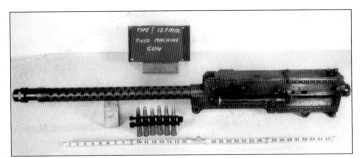

The Ki-44's initial wing armament consisted of a pair of 12.7 mm Ho-103 machine guns based on the US Model 1921 Browning aircraft gun. In the Otsu version of the fighter, this weapon also replaced the rifle-calibre cowling guns that were synchronised to fire through the propeller (*Picarella Collection*)

Groundcrew tackle the inertia starter of aircraft No 10 of the Kawasemi Butai as its pilot, WO Tokutaro Takakura, looks on from the cockpit. The Ki-44's massive engine is readily apparent, and the annular oil cooler within the cowling can be clearly seen (*Summer*)

fitted to the Ki-44's airframe with skilful streamlining. The aircraft also had a slab-sided fuselage behind the centre of gravity to improve stability. Pre-production models were capable of reaching speeds of 374 mph at an altitude of 12,860 ft, with an impressive rate of climb.

The design team had mated the large Ha-41 engine to the smallest airframe possible, with wings of only 161.46 sq ft creating a high wing loading of 30 lb/sq ft. Professor Hideo Itokawa had suggested the unusually small wing in order to address the Koku Hombu requirement for the aircraft to possess excellent gun platform characteristics. Professor Itokawa advised that a short span wing with strictly limited dihedral would reduce excessive lateral stability, whilst an increased fuselage profile area would achieve the directional stability required. During high-speed trials at Ota, senior Nakajima test pilot Hayashi had dived the aircraft 9840 ft to reach a speed of 528 mph, without experiencing any adverse handling characteristics whatsoever.

In a further departure from the norm for JAAF fighters, the new aircraft was relatively heavily armed. The Ki-27 had only two synchronised 7.7 mm rifle-calibre machine guns firing through the propeller, and early examples of the Ki-44's contemporary, the Ki-43, had the same limited armament (although by the outbreak of the Pacific War the Ki-43 was armed with either one or two 12.7 mm machine guns). Pre-production models of the Shoki introduced wing armament in the form of two 12.7 mm Army Type 1 Ho-103 machine guns firing to a muzzle velocity of 2657 ft/sec at 900 rounds per minute, with 250 rounds of belted ammunition in each wing. The Ki-44 also retained the then-standard JAAF fighter armament of two synchronised Army Type 89 kai 7.7 mm machine guns (with 500 rounds each) in the upper cowling firing through the propeller.

Another innovation to benefit the Ki-44 was the fitting of special Fowler-type wing flaps which, as well as providing the aircraft with additional lift for take-off and landing, could be used in flight to decrease the turning circle during combat. To facilitate this, the flaps were operated by two buttons on the top of control column. These were often mistaken for gun firing buttons. These devices became popularly known as a 'butterfly' flaps. Some Japanese sources state that they were first fitted to the 12th limited production machine serial number 112 following development for the Ki-43, which means that the aircraft supplied to the Kawasemi Butai lacked the flaps. However, it seems more probable that they were installed from the outset on all Ki-44s. The prototype aircraft had been constructed in August 1940, while the butterfly flaps were first introduced on the 11th Ki-43 pre-production aircraft

Three Ki-44 pre-production aircraft of the Kawasemi Butai's 2nd Hentai have their engines started up at Saigon in preparation for a sortie. The aircraft with the single yellow tail stripe is flown by the Hentai leader Capt Susumu Jinbo, while the Ki-44s of his two wingmen display two and three stripes respectively. The fighter furthest from the camera is a Ki-27 (*Summer*)

serial number 4311, which was constructed during that same month. In other words, the technology was an integral part of the Ki-44 design, and the flaps' success was exploited to improve the Ki-43.

In addition to Commander Sakagawa, the pilots assigned to the Kawasemi Butai were Capts Susumu Jinbo and Yasuhiko Kuroe, 1Lt Shunji Sugiyama, WOs Etsuji Mitsumoto, Tokutaro Takakura and Naosuke Okada and MSgts Takao Ito and Satoshi Tanaka. The Chutai was organised into three Hentai (Flights) of three aircraft each, commanded by Sakagawa, Jinbo and Kuroe respectively.

The 'chosen ones' had little time to familiarise themselves with the new aircraft before being ordered to move to Saigon in French Indochina (occupied by the Japanese in 1940). The 47th left Tachikawa on 3 December 1941 for Canton in China, where it learned of the outbreak of hostilities on 8 December. The following day the unit moved on to Saigon to be assigned to the Southern Area Army's direct command in preparation for combat operations. The Ki-44s were hastily camouflaged with brown paint to match the predominant earth colour of the region, before being committed to battle. The insignia chosen for the new unit – the design on the Yamaga-ryu drum used to signal the attack of the 47 Ronin – was painted beneath the cockpit of each fighter.

From Saigon the squadron moved on to Don Muang, in Thailand, on 24 December 1941, but Sakagawa and two other pilots suffered mechanical problems en route, resulting in the unit being reduced to just six serviceable aircraft. The move had been prompted by disastrous bomber attacks against Rangoon on 23 December, where the aggressiveness of the Allied fighter defence – Tomahawks of the American Volunteer Group (AVG, the famous 'Flying Tigers') and the Brewster Buffalo fighters of the RAF's No 67 Sqn – had taken the Japanese by surprise.

Although requested to participate in the next wave of air attacks on Rangoon by providing a potentially lethal top cover, Sakagawa had to scrub the mission for the 47th because the Ki-44 had insufficient range to fly such distances, and he could not risk using the rough and limited staging fields at Raheng and Phitsanulok. The experimental

Capt Yasuhiko Kuroe (the 3rd Hentai leader) taxis out at Saigon in his pre-production Ki-44 – the eighth prototype aircraft. Drop tanks extended the Shoki's limited range, but the improvised airstrips proved challenging for the fast-landing fighter (*Arawasi*)

A Ki-44 of the 47th Chutai's Kawasemi Butai taxis out across a rain-soaked airstrip in South-East Asia as groundcrew wave farewell. This unit deployed nine prototype and pre-production aircraft for testing in combat operations from the beginning of the Pacific War (*Summer*)

unit was therefore relegated to protecting the bombers as they staged through Don Muang on their way to bomb Rangoon.

In early January 1942 the 47th had its first taste of what was to become a common theme for the JAAF fighter units when it was suddenly switched to support air operations over Malaya. The 47th moved to Kuantan, on the east coast of Malaya, and on 15 January flew its first mission over Singapore when the Ki-44s joined Ki-43 'Oscars' of the 59th Sentai and Ki-27 'Nates' of the 1st Sentai escorting bombers raiding Tengah and Sembawang.

Kuroe, Jinbo and two wingmen were flying together when they spotted the Buffalo of 26-year-old New Zealander Plt Off Greville 'Butch' Hesketh of No 243 Sqn leading a section of No 488 Sqn Buffaloes up against the bombers. Kuroe made a diving attack on the Buffalo followed by Jinbo, both pilots scoring hits and then using the Ki-44's power to climb away. Kuroe attacked the disabled enemy aircraft again, and after five bursts of fire the Buffalo was shot down. Seriously wounded in the attack, Hesketh managed to crash-land beside the oil tanks near Alexandra Hospital, but he was dead by the time rescuers reached his wrecked aircraft. The Ki-44s were not recognised, being identified instead as 'Navy Type O' (Zero) fighters.

On the night of 20 January a bombing raid on Kuantan by Hudsons of No 8 Sqn RAAF resulted in four of the 47th's Ki-44s being damaged. Six days later Kuroe and Jinbo participated in the interception of a mixed force of RAF bombers that were attempting to destroy a large Japanese convoy approaching Endau. Kuroe, who had been aloft for some time, appears not to have attacked until Jinbo joined him. Of the ten Vildebeests lost over Endau by the RAF, the 47th claimed two, together with the No 232 Sqn Hurricane of Flt Sgt J Fleming.

By the end of January only one Ki-44 was serviceable, seriously limiting the unit's further participation in the air operations leading to the fall of Singapore. During the fighting Kuroe had claimed three RAF Hurricanes shot down. After a period of refit and repair, four aircraft had been returned to serviceability by 8 February, which meant that the unit could help in the provision of air cover for the Japanese landings on Singapore Island. No further victories were scored, however.

On 9 February the 47th was ordered to prepare to participate in the final air attacks on the RAF's

Burma airfields, and ten days later the four serviceable aircraft were flown to an ex-RAF dispersal field at Mudon, south of Moulmein in south-eastern Burma, where they were able to refuel with aviation fuel left behind by the British. The unit was assigned to Gen Eiryo Obata's 5th Air Division, which was planning to conduct a knockout blow against Mingaladon airfield on the outskirts of Rangoon.

Five days after the 47th's arrival, the airfield was strafed by Allied fighters, which set one of the Ki-44s on fire, destroying it. The following day (the 25th), the three remaining Ki-44s, piloted by Sakagawa, Mitsumoto and Kuroe, participated in a fighter sweep over Mingaladon with 44 'Nates' from the 50th and 77th Sentai. Three AVG Tomahawks and a single RAF Hurricane from No 17 Sqn, flown by American pilot Sgt J F 'Tex' Barrick, contested the sweep. A confused and swirling dogfight resulted in AVG and RAF claims for five 'Nates' shot down.

The Japanese pilots stated that they had been in combat with at least 20 fighters, and claimed no fewer than 16 shot down, two of which were credited to the Ki-44 pilots. In fact neither side had lost a single aircraft. Barrick was attacking a 'Nate' (which he claimed destroyed) when Sakagawa jumped him. As he tried to evade his opponent with a tight turn, one of the Hurricane's gun panels came open, causing the aircraft to 'flick' in the air. Barrick believed this had saved his life, for Sakagawa's Ki-44 was in a perfect firing position behind him. Unable to follow the Hurricane's sudden turn, the Japanese pilot dived away instead, followed by the remaining two Shokis. Barrick's Hurricane received no hits in the encounter, while the Ki-44s returned to Moulmein to refuel and re-arm.

That afternoon the Japanese struck Mingaladon again, this time with 12 Kawasaki Ki-48 'Lily' bombers from the 8th Sentai, escorted once more by the 'Nates' of the 50th and 77th Sentai and the three Ki-44s of the 47th. The JAAF force was met by AVG Tomahawks and 12 Hurricanes from Nos 17 and 135 Sqns. None of the Allied pilots reported seeing the new Japanese fighters during their engagements and, as had previously been the case, if the Ki-44s had indeed been noticed they were identified as 'Navy Zeros'. The Ki-44s were flying in line astern, with Sakagawa in the lead, when a Tomahawk suddenly attacked him in a gunnery run from his left. Evading this attack by skilfully jinking his machine, Sakagawa quickly latched onto another Tomahawk. Mitsumoto briefly pursued a second Tomahawk before being attacked by a third AVG fighter. Kuroe was flying too far behind to intervene, but he saw the encounter;

'This was the most dangerous moment, because Sakagawa and Mitsumoto were attacking and could not look around, so they did not see the enemy fighter that was positioned outside the battle area which now came in to attack. I went after him, but I was not fast enough. The enemy fired at Mitsumoto, then turned upside down and got out of the battlefield by diving fast.'

Mitsumoto's aircraft had been hit and he had been wounded in the attack, but he was able to return safely to Moulmein.

These operations had taken their toll on the Ki-44s, and their pilots were somewhat dissatisfied with the performance of the aircraft on operations, complaining about the lack of visibility from the cockpit, high landing speed and lack of manoeuvrability. These were pilots with combat experience in the nimble Ki-27, and they had watched the

Although he played a key part in the Ki-44's operational debut with the 47th Chutai, Maj Yasuhiko Kuroe was not an enthusiast of the aircraft, and he went on to fly the Ki-43 'Oscar' with the 64th Sentai in Burma. He survived the war with a total of 51 aerial victories to his name, and subsequently served postwar in the JASDF (*Henry Sakaida*)

participating sentais equipped with these familiar aircraft engaging the Allied fighters in classic dogfights throughout the campaign to date. On the other hand, the new fighter's high speed when diving, excellent roll rate and heavy armament were appreciated.

As a result, even before the experimental assignment of the Kawasemi Butai had ended, the Koku Hombu decided to authorise the limited production of a further 40 Ki-44s after considering it to be suitable as an anti-bomber or interceptor fighter. These first limited production aircraft, designated Ki-44-Is, were fitted with the Ha-41 engine. The first four (serial numbers 111-114) were ferried to the 47th in Burma as much needed reinforcements immediately after their completion in January and February 1942. The 47th's original brown camouflage had been deemed unsuccessful over the verdant landscapes of South-East Asia. Indeed, it highlighted the new fighter's slightly Buffalo-like appearance, causing several near-miss 'friendly fire' incidents. Consequently, the reinforcement Ki-44s were painted a dark olive green.

On 4 March four Ki-44s of the 47th conducted a sweep over the Sittang area, encountering four Bristol Blenheim I bombers of Nos 45 and 113 Sqns that had sortied from Magwe to attack targets in the same area. In their first pass, the Ki-44s damaged all four bombers, before concentrating on the Blenheim I piloted by Flt Lt F S Lee. Three of the Shokis repeatedly attacked the bomber from the rear, whilst the fourth, flown by Sakagawa, made a head-on run at it, firing into the cockpit. Lee was mortally wounded in this attack and the Blenheim I crashed 60 miles east of Pegu. The Ki-44s followed it down and strafed the wreckage. Only the air gunner, Sgt L Walker, survived, managing to return on foot.

On 21 March the 47th joined a formation of 52 Mitsubishi Ki-21 'Sally' bombers, escorted by 14 Ki-43s of the 64th Sentai, on a raid against the RAF/AVG airfield at Magwe, where there was a concentration of Allied aircraft. A second wave of ten Mitsubishi Ki-30 'Ann' light bombers, escorted by 14 Ki-27s, followed. In response, six Hurricanes and three AVG Tomahawks rose to challenge the JAAF formations in a series of confusing dogfights over the airfield. During this fighting 1Lt Shunji Sugiyama of the 47th became the unit's first combat fatality when he was shot down and killed. The remaining Ki-44s moved into Pegu, in Burma, at the end of March.

Following the raid on Tokyo on 18 April 1942 by Col Jimmy Doolittle's B-25 Mitchell bombers, which had taken off from the carrier USS *Hornet* (CV-8), the 47th was ordered to return to Japan. Seven days later the unit left Burma for the Homeland. The combat debut of Nakajima's Shoki was over.

Capt Kuroe did not return with the unit, having been transferred to the 64th Sentai on 24 April and appointed commander of its 3rd Chutai as a replacement for Capt Katsumi Anma, who had been killed on 8 April. Kuroe would have a successful career with this unit, becoming one of the 64th's leading aces with a tally of more than 30 aerial victories. In January 1944 he was transferred to the JAAF's Air Inspection Department, where, as a major, he evaluated experimental aircraft and new weapons systems, including large-calibre cannon and air-to-air rockets, during operational sorties against B-29s.

DEBUT IN CHINA

By the middle of 1942 the British had been driven out of Burma by the Japanese, but the air link between India and China had not been cut. Both sides consolidated and regrouped, whilst US forces inducted the AVG and made its leader, the iconic Claire C Chennault, the general in charge of its successor unit, the China Air Task Force (CATF). Inter-Allied suspicions between China, the USA and Great Britain, and inter-service differences between Chennault and his superior, the Anglophobe US Army Gen Joseph Stilwell, were to have a lasting negative impact on overall Allied strategy in the China-Burma-India (CBI) theatre.

Initially, Chennault was able to proceed with his plans to build up US and Chinese air power within China in order to interdict Japan's lines of communications in the South China Sea and ultimately to threaten the Japanese Homeland. With the assimilation of the AVG into the USAAF, Chennault had 51 ex-AVG Tomahawks and 20 P-40E Warhawks, of which just 29 were fit for operations. Fortunately for the Allies, Japan also paused in this theatre to lick its wounds and consider how best to proceed.

In December 1942 the Japanese Imperial General Headquarters advised the China Expeditionary Army that its strategy for continued operations in China was under 'grave consideration'. The HQ's instructions equivocated on the situation that whilst air operations were to be conducted only as the situation demanded, every effort was to be made to destroy the rapidly increasing enemy air forces. Further air operations in China would not be planned in detail until the first phase of the campaign in the Pacific had been completed. Offensive air operations there were not envisaged to be resumed until after the spring of 1943, and in the meantime were to be conducted within their present boundaries. In other words, a defensive posture was to be effectively maintained. Pursuant to this policy, the China Expeditionary Army was to arrange for the deployment of Type 2 (Ki-44 Shoki) fighters to each of the frontline airfields in north, central and south China as soon as possible.

By the end of 1942, only 40 limited production Ki-44-Is and 83 mass production Ki-44-IIs had left the Nakajima factory. These were delivered primarily to Homeland defence squadrons and the Akeno flying training school so as to train the pilots needed for the new fighter.

The first JAAF unit in China to receive the Ki-44 was the 33rd Sentai, based at Canton, but only five aircraft were delivered at the beginning of 1943 (according to some sources these arrived in the autumn of 1942). This famous fighter unit was predominantly equipped with Ki-43 'Oscars', but a shotai (flight) of Shokis was formed for air defence duties over the Wuchang area. Little is known about their deployment or exploits, and it appears that the 33rd Sentai did not receive any further Ki-44s after the initial delivery, or continue with their use beyond the spring of 1943.

On 1 April 1943 the 33rd deployed two of its Shokis, together with six 'Oscars', in a joint attack on Hengyang and Lingling, together with four 'Oscars' from the 25th Sentai. These 12 Japanese aircraft strafed the empty Hengyang airstrip before being jumped upon their arrival over Lingling by 14 P-40s (reported as more than 20) of the 75th Fighter Squadron. Although at a disadvantage, taken by surprise and outnumbered, the JAAF pilots optimistically claimed four USAAF fighters shot down. The Warhawk pilots reported engaging more than 30 Japanese fighters, and claimed five, but the participating Ki-44s were not specifically identified as a new type. Four pilots of the 25th and one from the 33rd (WO Kameo Okada) were reported lost, with Capt Barnum from the 75th FS also being killed in a collision with one of the Japanese fighters.

On 31 May the CO of the 33rd Sentai, Maj Akira Watanabe, led his small flight of Ki-44s to intercept nine B-24 bombers of the 374th and 425th Bomb Squadrons of the 308th Bomb Group that were attacking their base airfield at Kingmen, near Ichang. The bombers were escorted by several groups of Warhawks, which had become separated in bad weather on the approach to the target area. Only nine P-40s, flown by Capt John R Alison, CO of the 75th FS/23rd FG, fellow American Lt Charlie 'Chuck' Tucker and seven Chinese pilots, managed to stay with the bombers. They were at 16,000 ft and heading down through holes in the cloud base at 9000 ft when Watanabe's quartet of Ki-44s began climbing out of them.

'They could out-climb us and were passing me going up', Capt Alison later reported. 'There were three of them, and how they got up there so fast I'll never figure out, but they came in towards the bombers from the side and above'.

As Alison pulled up and began firing wildly at the three Ki-44s boring in towards the bombers, a fourth Shoki, flown by the 1st Chutai leader, Capt Yatsuto Ohtsubo, had climbed up below him and began shooting at him. Alison's P-40 was badly damaged in this attack, and he called to Tucker for help or 'I'm gone!' Whilst Ohtsubo was concentrating on his target, 1Lt Hsi-Lan Tsang slipped in behind his Ki-44 and shot him down. Although he managed to bail out, Ohtsubo was badly wounded and subsequently died. Alison managed to land at Kunming with his rudder hanging from a single cable, both tyres shot out and several hits to the armour plate behind his seat, including an armour-piercing bullet stuck in the plate between his shoulder blades.

MORE UNITS CONVERT

During the autumn and winter of 1942 the 85th and 87th Sentais had commenced transitioning to the new Ki-44 at Hailing, in Manchuria, as component units of the 13th Air Brigade of the 2nd Air Division. This had not proven an easy task, as the units made the transition

The Ki-44 was at first restricted to pilots with at least 1000 hours of flying time because of its tricky handling characteristics, but it was later found that younger pilots who had not been instilled with the extensive aerobatic training of earlier cadres could manage the aircraft perfectly well, so the restriction was removed. This view emphasises the Shoki's enormous engine (*Summer*)

directly from the obsolete Ki-27, and at the time only those pilots with at least 1000 hours of flying time were deemed sufficiently capable of handling the Ki-44. The Sentai had not only to wring out the Shoki's very different performance characteristics, but also to adapt personnel imbued with the concept of horizontal manoeuvre dogfighting to a new concept of hit-and-run tactics using the aircraft's superior speed, dive and climb capabilities.

The emphasis for the Japanese fighter regiments in Manchuria was air defence of the border against possible Soviet incursions, and the units practised rapid take-off and climb to altitude, followed by the interception of incoming formations. Perhaps because of the nature of this transition, and the practice involved, the 85th became one of the most proficient and successful users of the Ki-44 in air-to-air combat.

In the meantime, Imperial General Headquarters had firmed up their intentions for air operations in China, and on 17 February 1943 it issued instructions for a summer air offensive against US forces. The China Expeditionary Army was ordered 'to make every effort' to strengthen its air operations in order to destroy enemy air strength, and to prevent bombing raids from being launched against Japan from air bases in China. As part of the plan it was decided that two fighter and two bomber regiments would be allocated as reinforcements to the 3rd Air Division, which had moved its headquarters to the Wu-Han area in mid-January 1943.

In June 1943 the 85th and 87th Sentais were ordered to transfer to China in compliance with these Imperial General Headquarters requirements, but almost immediately the 87th was instructed to return to Japan. In July the 85th, commanded by Maj Goro Yamamoto, occupied the airfields around the 'three cities' of Wuchang, Hankow and Henyang (Wu-Han area), in central China.

The unit had a relatively small complement of experienced and Ki-44 proficient pilots, and they were placed under the direct command of the 3rd Air Division (Hikoshidan) Headquarters. The more capable 2nd Chutai, under Capt Yukiyoshi Wakamatsu, was almost immediately detached to Canton in south China. Small detachments were also sent to Hong Kong to provide aerial defence of this strategic location. Thereafter, the 85th regularly shuttled formations between Hankow, Canton and Hong Kong, using these staging operations to maintain attacks against US air bases in south-west China, as well as providing local defence against US incursions.

From the outset the sentai was stretched in both geographical deployment and mission, being required to provide an offensive air combat capability against US fighters and to undertake both day and night air defence of key locations. This resulted in relatively small numbers of aircraft being

This early Ki-44 (probably of the 85th Sentai in China) was flown by Sgt Tadashi Kikukawa, whose surname is represented by the personal emblem on the tail. This photograph appeared in the *Pacific War Pictorial No 24*, published by the Japanese newspaper *Mainichi* in November 1943. Sgt Kikukawa was killed in action over Suichuan on 12 February 1944 (*Summer*)

committed piecemeal to operations, with the burden falling on the most experienced pilots.

On 23 July 1943 the Japanese began the first phase of their summer offensive against US airfields in China, with major attacks against the nascent USAAF bases of Hengyang, Lingling and Kweilin by Ki-43s of the 25th and 33rd Sentais, escorting Ki-21 'Sally' bombers of the 58th and 60th Sentais from airfields in Indochina and Ki-48 'Lily' bombers of the 90th Sentai from Formosa (Taiwan). Throughout the campaign the JAAF proved adept at staging formations of aircraft through China from bases overseas to support or execute specific operations.

The appearance of the new Ki-44 in-theatre had not been lost on Chennault, although it continued to be reported in most encounters as a 'Zero' or sometimes a 'Hamp' (the A6M3 Type 32 version of the IJNAF Zero-sen, featuring clipped wings). 'It was a standard Japanese air blitz – bombers pounding our fields after midnight and fighter sweeps by daylight, with a few bombers as P-40 bait', Chennault noted. 'This time they had two new fighter types – the "Oscar Mk II", a faster and more heavily armed version of their old stand-by, and the "Tojo" [Ki-44], a stubby, barrel-bodied fighter that looked not unlike a Thunderbolt. It could out-run the P-40, and was the best all round fighter in China skies that summer'.

During these attacks the 85th was supposed to provide top cover to the fighter sweeps, with the expectation of being able to pick off the intercepting P-40s using the hit-and-run tactics its pilots had pioneered. On the morning of 24 July eight Ki-44s, led by Yukiyoshi Wakamatsu, took off from Canton to conduct a preliminary fighter sweep over Kweilin. The fighters caught the P-40s of the 74th FS/23rd FG as they were getting into the air in response to one of several 'jing baos' (air raid warnings) that day.

Also on the field were the newly arrived P-38 Lightnings of the 449th FS, and one of these, flown by Capt Walter A Smith (a P-40 pilot

This Ki-44-II Ko was said to be one of the aircraft flown by 85th Sentai ace Yukiyoshi Wakamatsu, and it was photographed in China during 1943. The Ki-44-II variant can be distinguished from the earlier Ko version by the prominent oil cooler beneath the cowling (*Yasuho Izawa via Hiroshi Umemoto*)

seconded from the 74th to lead the unit, as he had previously flown the P-38) was shot down shortly after take-off.

As they flashed across the airfield and into the P-40s, the Ki-44s were again identified as 'Zeros'. The combat occurred between 6000 and 7000 ft, and the 23rd FG leader, Col Bruce K Holloway, noted that the P-40s 'were just about on an even keel with the Zeros (sic), who were still hanging around and just flying individually'. The recurring tendency for some of the Japanese flyers to want to 'stick around' for a manoeuvring fight 'on the level' lost them the best advantage the Ki-44 offered, and two of the 85th's pilots were downed that morning.

Sgt Fumio Yonezu and a wingman made a gunnery run on the P-40 of 1Lt William B Hawkins, but the American pilot used the scattered cloud cover to evade the wingman and to get on the tail of Yonezu. The latter then tried to outrun the P-40 in level flight, but a second Warhawk flown by Lt Robert M Cage intervened in the pursuit. Hawkins was unable to fire at the Ki-44 with Cage in the way, but Cage had just one operable gun and was only able to damage Yonezu's aircraft. Eventually, Cage broke away and Yonezu took the chance to pull up into a steep climbing turn to the left in an attempt to regain altitude. Whilst performing this manoeuvre Hawkins managed to hit the Ki-44 in the left wing root with a short burst of fire from all six of his 0.50-cal machine guns as the fighter climbed. The Shoki immediately burst into flames. Yonezu bailed out of the burning aircraft, but his parachute and clothing were already on fire and he subsequently died from his injuries.

Wakamatsu claimed his first two kills over Kweilin that day, beginning a run of victories over US fighters in China, but it appears that the only USAAF loss was Smith's P-38. The US flyers claimed seven of the 'Tojos' shot down, reporting that only one had managed to escape.

Wakamatsu had joined the JAAF in 1930 as a NCO cadet. After training as a fighter pilot, he became a flying instructor and was commissioned as an officer in 1938. Despite his age (he was 32 years old) and flying experience, Wakamatsu had seen little combat prior to being appointed leader of the 85th's 2nd Chutai on his promotion to captain in August 1942. His exploits over China became legendary, however, and his marksmanship was considered to be as exceptional as his flying skill. Indeed, Wakamatsu acquired a reputation for claiming victories with single bursts of fire at long range.

The red-painted spinner (and possibly cowling ring) on his Ki-44 led to his soubriquet as the 'Red Nose Ace' or 'Captain Red Ace'. Japanese propaganda exploited Wakamatsu's reputation, and his radio transmissions made during combat were sometimes broadcast. So dangerous was Wakamatsu considered to be in the air that the Chinese Nationalist (Kuomintang) government was alleged to have offered a large monetary reward of 20,000 Customs Gold Units (the equivalent of $45,200 Chinese national yuan, or dollars, at that time) for his head. Wakamatsu perfectly exploited the best qualities of the Ki-44 with hit-and-run tactics executed with surgical precision.

In addition to Wakamatsu, the other top-scoring ace of the 85th Sentai was WO Rikio Shibata, a 26-year-old flyer who had claimed 14 victories whilst serving as a corporal pilot in the 11th Sentai during the Nomonhan fighting against the Soviet air force in 1939. Having

Capt Yukiyoshi Wakamatsu of the 85th Sentai was a skilled exponent of the Ki-44 over China, and he is seen here wearing summer flying kit and standing by the tail of his fighter probably at Canton. Dubbed the 'Red Nose Ace', his prowess was so well-known that the Chinese government reputedly put a reward on his head (*Yasuho Izawa via Hiroshi Umemoto*)

joined the 1st Chutai of the 85th in March 1941, Shibata held the rank of sergeant major by the summer of 1943. Promoted to warrant officer in December 1943, by the time of his death in action on 18 December 1944 Shibata's final score was estimated to be 27 victories, of which at least 12 were scored with the Ki-44.

On 30 July Capt Yoshioki Nakahara led nine 3rd Chutai Ki-44s, together with Ki-43s from the 25th and 33rd Sentais, as escorts for 'Sally' bombers attacking Hengyang. The Shokis approached the target separately by flying to the west and then south, converging with the main force before it reached Hengyang. The US/Chinese warning net monitored the approach of the Japanese formations and informed the defending P-40 pilots from the 23rd FG of their movements. With both Japanese formations in sight, the Warhawks feinted towards the Ki-44s, but then turned abruptly to strike at the bombers. According to the pilots of the 85th Sentai, they successfully 'bounced' the P-40s as they approached the main force, claiming four shot down and two probables.

Two Warhawks did indeed go down, Lt W S Epperson of the 75th FS being killed and 1Lt Howard H Krippner of the 76th FS bailing out. The P-40 pilots claimed four bombers and three fighters destroyed, as well as six probables, but no Ki-44s were lost in the engagement.

The tactics employed by the 85th Sentai during the late summer of 1943 saw Ki-44s being regularly shuttled between Canton and Hankow, conducting sweeps over USAAF airfields on their way and also employing feints in order to lure the P-40s up to fight at a disadvantage. Chennault recognised these tactics;

'Formations of from 20 to 50 fighters shuttled over our fields between Hankow and Canton at 30,000 ft all day, trying to lure the P-40s way upstairs.'

His response was to order his bomber forces, with fighter escorts, to attack the Japanese airfields at Hankow and Canton in order to force the JAAF fighters into a defensive posture down at the operating altitudes favoured by the American fighters. The first raids were not as successful in neutralising the Japanese fighter forces as he had hoped, and bomber losses were heavy. The Japanese pilots had studied and refined their tactics for tackling the B-24s, taking advice from their comrades in Burma who had already fought the bombers, and the P-40 escorts were ineffective in intervening against the interceptions.

On 20 August Wakamatsu was able to score again using the dive-and-zoom tactics perfected by the sentai. At least 20 aircraft from the 85th conducted another fighter sweep over Kweilin that morning and, alerted to the incoming raid, 14 P-40s took off to intercept them. However, they found that the Japanese fighter sweep was being flown at what they estimated to be 30,000-35,000 ft. The Ki-44s cruised with impunity above the P-40s in wide circles, seizing opportunities to make diving attacks against them and then zooming up and away again (zooming was forbidden in the Ki-44 pilot's manual, but this did not seem to impede the 85th's tactics). During these attacks Wakamatsu downed two P-40s in quick succession, the first to fall being flown by Capt Truman O Jeffreys, followed by the fighter of Lt Mao Y K. Both men were killed.

As the Warhawks attempted to make gunnery runs on the Japanese aircraft attacking their compatriots, the Ki-44s pulled into fast, steep climbs to evade them. Capt Arthur W Cruikshank Jr claimed two of the Shokis shot down but none were actually lost. Col Bruce Holloway went after another Ki-44 that was making a run on Maj Norval Bonawitz's Warhawk, but the Japanese fighter 'pulled into a climb that carried him right out of Holloway's firing range'.

Another successful 85th Sentai pilot involved in the fighting was Akiyoshi Nomura, a protégé of Wakamatsu, who was to claim at least ten victories in China. He had participated in the 23 July 1943 sweep over Kweilin. On 20 August the engine of his Ki-44 had suddenly stopped running, and he resolved to kill himself rather than bail out or force-land in enemy territory. As he dived towards the ground, his engine suddenly picked up and began running normally again, allowing him to return safely to base.

Sgt Maj Misao Ohkubo was yet another notable Ki-44 ace who also flew in the 85th's 2nd Chutai at this time, claiming at least eight victories over China.

On 21 August, warning of another Japanese fighter sweep coming in over Hengyang from Canton disrupted American plans for a raid on Hankow. Two formations of P-40s, led by Col Holloway and Maj Bob Costello of the 76th FS, took off and began climbing hard for altitude, listening to updates about the sweep from the warning net over their radios. While the Warhawk pilots were still climbing Wakamatsu's eight Ki-44s suddenly bounced the American formation out of the sun, diving through it and showering it with their jettisoned drop tanks.

One of the Shoki pilots got in behind a P-40 flown by 1Lt Harvey G 'Nightmare' Elling and began firing at him, rounds passing over the Warhawk's wings on either side of Elling's canopy. The American pilot evaded with a proven manoeuvre against the Japanese 'Oscar' of pushing the stick fully forward and to the right and going into a 'split-S' dive until 300 mph was reached, at which point Elling pulled up hard. As he did this he discovered that the Ki-44 was still close behind him on his tail, and still shooting. He repeated the same 'split-S' manoeuvre a second time, but the Ki-44 kept with him, firing short, controlled bursts at his P-40. A third attempt brought Elling low over the ground, with the Shoki still pursuing and firing.

WO Akiyoshi Nomura smiles from the cockpit of his Ki-44 in China. Another ace of the 85th Sentai and a protégé of Capt Wakamatsu, Nomura fought over China in 1943-44, achieving ten kills. The Army Type 89 telescopic gunsight fitted to this aircraft has a rubber eyepiece and a protective cap that could be opened from the cockpit before combat. The use of this type of sight reduced the pilot's situational awareness, and a reflector type gunsight was introduced in later versions of the Ki-44 (*Yasuho Izawa via Hiroshi Umemoto*)

Having by now realised that the Japanese pilot was flying a better aircraft, and that it was only a matter of time before he was shot down, Elling glanced back anxiously but was relieved to see that his assailant was finally giving up the chase and turning away. He noticed the outline of the aircraft as it turned, and realised that it was not 'the usual "Zeke" or "Oscar"'. Elling subsequently wrote;

'Shortly after this encounter, information came to us of a new fast and heavily armed fighter which could outperform the P-40 due to its large engine and sturdy elliptical wings. It was called the "Tojo". I had seen it!'

One P-40 was destroyed during this combat, 1Lt Donald Hedrick of the 76th FS bailing out safely, whilst his comrades claimed to have shot down five 'Zeros'. No 85th Sentai pilots were lost, however.

On 26 August Wakamatsu was again in action over Tien Ho airfield, near Canton, against P-40s of the 76th and 16th FSs. Capt J M 'Willie' Williams of the 76th noted the speed at which the Japanese 'Zeros' climbed from the field as the USAAF formation approached;

'The Japanese had new fighters in the air. They were larger and faster than what I had seen before. One got on my tail. I dived and turned left, which would normally shake the Zeros that I had seen before. This one stayed with me, but could not lead [e.g. turn tighter to aim off] me enough to shoot me down.'

Williams managed to evade his pursuer by flying into cloud, emerging to see another P-40 being attacked by a 'Tojo'. He fired at this one, causing it to break off and pull into a vertical climb, but the other Warhawk, flown by Lt Robert Sweeney, was forced to crash-land. Williams fired at the 'Tojo' at the top of its climb and claimed to have hit it, seeing the fighter roll over with black smoke pouring out of it and dive into the ground. Sweeney also reported that the 'Tojo' had crashed close to where he had come down, but no 85th Sentai pilots were reported killed on that day. It is possible that the pilot managed to bail out. The Warhawk pilots on this mission claimed five 'Tojos' shot down and three probables.

It is not difficult to understand why the Ki-44 made little impression on the enemy until late August 1943. Earlier in the year it had been committed only in small numbers, and it had taken the 85th several weeks to settle into the combat environment in China and to get the best from its new fighter. But another contributory factor was probably the introduction of a more powerful engine fitted in the Ki-44-II series, which had commenced production in modest numbers in September 1942. The fighter's new powerplant was the Nakajima Ha-109 14-cylinder two-row two-stage supercharged radial air-cooled engine, rated at 1520 hp.

Mass production of the new version began in January 1943, and by August of that year almost 250 had been built. In addition to the Ha-109 engine, the design team introduced other improvements to the aircraft, including greater fuel capacity and better hydraulic systems and landing gear, as well as incorporating thicker armour plating to protect the pilot and improved leak-proofing of the fuel tanks.

ALLIED EXAMINATION

Some confusion exists as to when the Allies first got a close look at a Shoki, albeit a crashed one. Capt Richard P Reinsch of the Allied Technical Air Intelligence Unit (ATAIU) reported examining the wreckage of WO Okada's 33rd Sentai Ki-44 (one of the early production models) after it had been downed over Lingling on 1 April 1943. However, fellow ATAIU officer Capt Carl G Nelson subsequently maintained that the first 'Tojo' to be examined in China was Sgt Maj Shigeharu Sasaki's Ki-44, which was shot down near Kweilin on 5 October 1943, following

1Lt Harvey G. Elling's report of encountering new fighter aircraft over Hengyang in August.

When ATAIU published a comparison of the 'Tojo' with the IJNAF's Mitsubishi J2N Raiden ('Jack') interceptor as late as April 1944, the details represented the earlier model Ki-44-I. Nevertheless, two ATAIU reports disclose that Sgt Maj Sasaki's aircraft was indeed a Ki-44-II, with 'armament converted to four 12.7 mm machine guns in place of the two 12.7 mm and two 7.7 mm machine guns of the earlier model examined. The armour plate was a different type, and quite a bit heavier than previously examined'.

A US Intelligence document from January 1944 noted that the 'Tojo' 'was not so manoeuvrable as the "Zeke" or "Oscar", but much faster in a dive, climb and level flight', and that the Ki-44 Pilot Manual 'listed restrictions on spins, snap-rolls, quick turns, sudden zooms at high speed and accelerations greater than 5 g. Combat reports indicate that these restrictions are not respected by Jap[anese] pilots!'

Despite the efforts made by the JAAF, the first phase of its 1943 air offensive in China was deemed ultimately unsuccessful in preventing the US air forces from increasing their materiel strength in south-west China. For the second and third phases of the offensive it was decided to concentrate air units in south China and Indochina for an increased intensity of attacks on US bases in the Yunnan and Kweilin areas. By the beginning of September the JAAF had combined the main strengths of two fighter regiments and two heavy bomber regiments in Indochina, supported by the high-flying and fast reconnaissance Mitsubishi Ki-46 Type 100 'Dinah' command reconnaissance aircraft of the 18th Dokuritsu Dai Shijugo Chutai (Independent Air Squadron).

The Japanese suffered a severe blow to their plans on 9 September when the MC-21 (a transport version of the Ki-21 'Sally') carrying the 3rd Air Division commander, Lt Gen Nakazono Moritaka, and his staff to their new headquarters at Canton was shot down south of the city by 2Lt Billie M Beardsley. Assigned to the P-38-equipped 449th FS, Beardsley, who was flying one of four Lightnings that had just completed a successful dive-bombing mission against shipping at Whampoa, came across the transport as he egressed the target area. The 1st Air Brigade Headquarters at Canton had issued a warning for friendly aircraft to remain clear of the Canton area in response to the Whampoa attack, but it appears that Moritaka's aircraft did not receive, or act upon, this warning. The MC-21 crashed on an island in the Pearl River estuary, killing all on board.

Although Maj Gen Rokuro Imanishi quickly replaced Moritaka, this incident seriously compromised and undermined Japanese air operations for the rest of 1943. That same day the 85th's 3rd Chutai lost its leader when Capt Yoshioki Nakahara was shot down and killed over Tien Ho airfield by P-40s of the 74th FS. Capt Morio Nakamura replaced him.

On 10 September Wakamatsu led a Ki-44 formation against six more P-38s that were dive-bombing shipping in Whampoa harbour, but none were claimed. The P-38 pilots, however, claimed one 'Zero' destroyed and another damaged. No 85th Sentai pilots were reported lost.

Throughout the summer and autumn of 1943, the 85th had been sending small detachments of Ki-44s from Canton to operate from

Pilots of the 85th Sentai's 1st Chutai pose for a photograph at Canton in August 1943. The chutai leader, Capt Akira Horaguchi, is standing second from left in the back row, whilst the 85th's leading ace, Sgt Maj Rikio Shibata, is kneeling second from left in the front row. Shibata claimed a total of 27 victories, the majority in the Ki-44. The photo shows well the distinctive camouflage applied to many of the unit's 'Tojos' in China (*Yasuho Izawa*)

Kai Tak airfield in Kowloon, Hong Kong. Local people who saw these aircraft arriving knew that they were different to the IJNAF Zeros already there, and rumours spoke of a 'special squadron' that would punish the Americans for their attacks on the harbour and city. One Chinese eyewitness described the new aircraft as 'mottled brown like the skin of a snake or toad', while others recalled seeing black-painted fighters.

The Japanese Army had built a radar station on Hong Kong's tallest mountain – Tai Mo Shan (more than 3000 ft in height) – that was able to detect formations of aircraft at a theoretical range of 155 miles, thus providing some degree of early warning to the fighters based at Kai Tak.

On 1 December 1943, the newly created Chinese-American Composite Wing (CACW) flew its first mission in a strike on Hong Kong when 17 brand new P-40Ns escorted nine B-25s. As the formation approached Kowloon, five Ki-44s suddenly attacked but were driven off. One of them was claimed as a probable by B-25 gunner Sgt Wei.

That same day, the Kai Tak detachment executed a perfect bounce on six P-51As of the 76th FS, led by Col 'Tex' Hill, that were escorting Liberators on a raid against targets in Canton and Hong Kong. Over Hong Kong, the Mustang formation became dangerously strung out whilst climbing from 10,000 ft to 22,000 ft. As Hill turned the formation north, the Ki-44s bounced them from above and quickly shot down two Mustangs. Lt Bob Colbert bailed out of his stricken fighter whilst Capt Williams managed to belly land his badly damaged Mustang in a rice paddy north of Macao. Hill claimed to have damaged one of the 'Tojos' in return, but none were lost.

Capt Akira Horaguchi, the 1st Chutai leader of the 85th Sentai in China, stands with his groundcrew in front of his personal Ki-44. The 1st Chutai used white as their recognition colour, here applied to the propeller spinner and in the form of a broad white fuselage band, which indicated that Capt Horaguchi was chutai leader (*Yasuho Izawa via Hiroshi Umemoto*)

Upon his return to Kweilin, veteran ace 'Tex' Hill expressed doubt about the P-51's ability to fight the 'Tojo', stating, 'I don't think we can beat these new Japs in the air'. Chennault was unfazed, however, replying, 'Don't worry about it. Just hit them on the ground'.

The 85th Sentai was not overly impressed by the appearance of the first P-51 Mustangs in-theatre either. Wakamatsu had recorded in his diary on the day of his first P-51 kill that it had been like taking candy from a child, while another Japanese fighter pilot who had served in the CBI described them as no better than a P-40, but with less hitting power.

On 2 December the 85th flew an offensive sweep against Suichuan, meeting Warhawks of the 76th FS over the field. Two P-40Ks were shot down by the Ki-44s, although Lts Elmore P Bullock and Max Noftsger survived the experience. Noftsger shot down and killed Sgt Tamotsu Nishikawa of the 85th moments before he went down himself. USAAF pilots claimed one destroyed, one probable and two damaged.

Two days later six Ki-44s of the 85th bounced a morning patrol of P-40s from the 74th and 75th FS as they approached Changteh and shot down Lt Wallace Cousins of the 74th, who was able to bail out and return to his unit. The Japanese fighters repeated the performance in the afternoon, when 16 Ki-44s bounced more P-40s and downed Capt Paul Bell, CO of the 74th FS. The American pilots claimed five probables and four damaged in return during these encounters, although they had in fact killed the 85th's 1st Chutai commander,

Capt Horaguchi of the 85th Sentai poses in front of a newly delivered Ki-44-II Otsu (lacking wing armament), which has yet to be camouflaged. Horaguchi was killed in action over Changteh on 4 December 1943 (*Yasuho Izawa via Hiroshi Umemoto*)

Capt Akira Horaguchi. The identity of his attacker is unknown. Lt Hajime Saito was appointed to lead the 1st Chutai following Horaguchi's death.

On 6 December the CACW attacked Japanese positions near Changteh, with four B-25 Mitchells flying at 10,000 ft escorted by P-40s. Five 'silver' Ki-44s attacked the formation head on, one by one, pulling up over the B-25s as they fired, then rolling and diving away. Two bombers sustained damage but none were lost. The P-40s went after the Ki-44s and claimed one shot down and four probables, but none of the Japanese aircraft were lost.

Later in the day a second attack was mounted against the same target, and a mixed force of Ki-43s and Ki-44s engaged the CACW formation head on. The Japanese pilots shot down two Warhawks and damaged a third, Lt S Y Tan managing to bail out wounded but Lt Boyle being killed. B-25 gunner Sgt Wei, who had also made a claim over Hong Kong five days earlier, stated that he had downed a 'Tojo', but none were in fact lost.

The tactics adopted by Ki-44 pilots, which saw them attacking the bombers once and then rolling over and diving away on full power, were misleading, and possibly giving the impression to their foes of them being shot down.

The 1st Chutai of the 85th suffered a setback on 11 December. After raiding Suichuan and finding no US aircraft there, the formation returned to Nanchang, an airfield at the southern tip of Poyang Lake to the south-east of Hankow. Maj Elmer Richardson, guessing that the Japanese fighters had come from Nanchang, led nine Warhawks from the 74th and 75th FSs at Hengyang directly to the Japanese airfield and caught the returning Ki-44s in their landing pattern with their wheels and flaps down. Unable to defend themselves, the Shokis were quickly picked off by the American pilots, who claimed no fewer than six fighters destroyed. Sgt Maj Sakio Hade and Sgt Yoshio Sakagami both perished when their Shokis crashed.

Twelve days later, 15 Ki-44s from the 85th Sentai were scrambled from Canton to intercept an incoming raid of 308th BG B-24s, escorted by seven P-51s and 23 P-40s drawn from the 74th and 76th FSs of the 23rd FG and the 28th and 32nd Provisional FSs (PFSs) of the CACW. Lt S Y Hwang and K C Wang of the CACW were shot down and killed during the subsequent fighting. The raiders in turn claimed six Japanese fighters destroyed and six probables, although only Sgt Maj Hidesue Ikubo of the 85th was reported as being killed. He was the last pilot from the unit to die in combat in 1943.

During the aerial campaign over China in 1943, the 85th had had a total of 11 pilots killed in action, three of whom were officers (two of them chutai leaders), with several others being wounded and invalided home. These attritional losses of nearly 20 percent were more serious than at first they might have seemed, for relatively inexperienced replacement pilots were now being committed to operations at a time when Allied air attacks were increasing in their intensity. Indeed, the 85th found it necessary to operate a 4th 'training' Chutai equipped with Ki-43 'Oscars' where replacement pilots could improve their flying skills prior to being ordered to undertake combat missions in the more demanding Ki-44.

EAST INDIES AND BURMA

As noted at the end of chapter one, when the Ki-44-equipped 47th Dokuritsu Hiko Chutai had been hastily recalled to Japan after the Doolittle Raid, Capt Yasuhiko Kuroe did not go with it. Instead, he was transferred to the 64th Sentai in Burma as its 3rd Chutai leader. The 64th was one of the two sentais that had given the 'Oscar' its combat debut at the outbreak of hostilities with the Allies in December 1941, and the unit was to be equipped with this fighter throughout the war. Kuroe was to have a successful career and become an ace in the 64th, eventually claiming 30+ victories.

Despite the fact that Kuroe had expressed the view that the Ki-44 had not lived up to his expectations, on 4 May 1943, after missing a B-24 and F-4 photo-reconnaissance Lightning interception over Rangoon, he wrote in his wartime diary 'We need a Ki-44!' These feelings had been expressed by other 64th Sentai pilots who hoped that their Ki-43 Hayabusa fighters might be replaced with the Ki-44 after recently experiencing frustrating and unsuccessful combats with B-24s. It would be another five months, however, before the sentai had the opportunity to fly the Ki-44 in combat.

Four new Shokis ferried from Japan arrived at Mingaladon airfield, near Rangoon, on 11 October 1943, 64th Sentai pilots Lt Masayoshi Niwa, 2Lts Shiro Suzuki and Naoyuki Ito and WO Takahama having flown them there. Lt Suzuki crashed on landing, destroying the Ki-44 he was flying. The three remaining Shokis were then based at Mingaladon for the purpose of interception duties, but despite expectations, they were not particularly valued by pilots who had been imbued with the concept of using aerobatics and manoeuvre to achieve success in aerial combat.

The 64th Sentai received a small number of Ki-44s at the end of 1943 to augment the air defence capability over Rangoon in the face of increasing Allied bombing raids. Groundcrew of the 4th Chutai pose with the aircraft believed to have been flown by 2Lt Suzuki (*via Hiroshi Umemoto*)

The 20-victory ace Capt Saburo Nakamura tested one of the new Shokis in mock combat against a Ki-43 flown by Sgt Masahiro Ikeda. Nakamura attempted to dive and catch Ikeda, but the warrant officer was able to evade his gunnery runs each time. Nakamura was unable to get the 'Oscar' in his sights, and Ikeda subsequently expressed the opinion that the Ki-44 was 'nothing good'.

Despite his wish for the 64th to receive some Ki-44s, it appears that Kuroe never flew them in combat with the sentai, and, surprisingly, his successful interceptions of fast-flying RAF Mosquitos appear to have been achieved whilst at the controls of the Ki-43 'Oscar'. Nevertheless, by August 1944 the 64th Sentai was reported to have nine Ki-44s on strength with a 4th Chutai, these being flown from Rangoon airfields.

On 27 November 1943 2Lt Suzuki, flying one of the Ki-44s, was shot down and killed over Rangoon by P-51As from the 311th FG. His victor was probably 1Lt J J England of the 530th FS, who had fired a long burst at a 'Zeke' at 6800 ft and seen it explode. According to Japanese records Suzuki had been pursuing a P-51 when a second Mustang latched onto his tail and shot him down. Suzuki was flying the sole Ki-44 in a 64th Sentai formation that was otherwise made up of eight Ki-43s, the aircraft being led by Kuroe in the interception of a large USAAF bombing raid on the Insein workshops.

Four days later Lt Masayoshi Niwa avenged Suzuki's death when he claimed two P-51As from the 311th FG destroyed over Rangoon while flying a new Ki-44 that he had ferried in on 29 November. Only the Mustang flown by Lt Allan D Du Bose failed to return from the mission, however, and Niwa was the only claimant on this date.

Members of the 4 Field HQ of South-East Asia Command's Allied Technical Air Intelligence Unit (ATAIU) examine the remains of a 50th Sentai Ki-44 at Meiktila, in Burma. They were especially interested in acquiring data about the fighter's 40 mm Ho-301 cannon. This is the only known photograph to show a Ki-44 in the markings of this Burma-based Ki-43 unit (*via James F Lansdale*)

A small number of the Ki-44s were also supplied to the 50th Sentai, which was another predominantly 'Oscar'-equipped unit in Burma. Little is known about their use in-theatre, although they appear to have been deployed offensively from airfields in central Burma, and also during the Imphal campaign. There are a few scattered reports of encounters with Allied fighters, whose pilots, whilst noticing the new type, did not always identify it. For example, on the afternoon of 7 March 1944 P-51A Mustangs of the 1st Air Commando engaged six unidentified Japanese fighters taking off from Anisikan. The US pilots noticed that the aircraft had larger engines than Zero-sens, and could use their power to take evasive action. From the markings described these aircraft were possibly 50th Sentai Ki-44s.

The previous month, on 9 February, Flt Sgt R W G Cross of the RAF's No 136 Sqn had encountered several similar fighters over Buthidaung. In a dogfight and pursuit that resulted in damage to his own aircraft, he noted that the Ki-44s were able to keep up with him in level flight and had a climbing speed comparable to his Spitfire VIII;

'Having dived from a great height, my IAS (indicated air speed) was 320-340 mph, so I swung around and climbed up into the sun. I was followed by four bandits who kept up with me very well until I was forced to flatten out at 18,000 ft and fly level, weaving violently.'

Flt Sgt Cross' description of these aircraft in his combat report matches the Ki-44, and his observation of wing armament firing precludes the possibility that they were Ki-43 'Oscars'.

87TH IN BURMA

The 87th Sentai had been sent to the East Indies in December 1943 with about 40 Ki-44-II fighters to protect the vital oil refineries at Plaju and Sungai Gerong, in Sumatra. The unit was based at the airfield the Japanese called Gloembang, the pre-war name for Kota Gelumbang, which was the ex-Dutch airfield P2 at Palembang. It had three runways, one of which was 6500 ft in length and two of 4900 ft. Other JAAF units such as the 21st and 33rd Sentais, equipped with the Kawasaki Ki-45 'Nick' twin-engined fighter and Ki-43 'Oscar', respectively, also used Gloembang as a dispersion field for their main operations from Talang Betutuvii.

About half of the 87th's fighters were Ki-44-II Hei types, armed with four 12.7 mm machine guns, while the rest were Ki-44-II Otsu with two synchronised 12.7 mm weapons firing from the cowling and provision for two 40 mm cannon in the wings.

The 87th's pilots settled into a somewhat dull routine of flying patrols and performing practice interceptions, which meant that they had little opportunity to gain real combat experience in their Ki-44s. Small detachments were also sent to Port Blair, in the Andaman Islands, to provide air defence and interception capability against intruding RAF bombers and photo-reconnaissance aircraft.

In May 1944 the 87th Sentai moved from Sumatra to bases in Burma for the ground offensive against Imphal, codenamed Operation *U-Go*, as reinforcements for the 'Oscar' units supporting the army. The reason for this deployment was, in part, to provide pilots that were eager for action with the opportunity to gain combat experience against the latest

Allied aircraft types. The sentai arrived in Burma on 8 May, staging to the various satellite airfields around Meiktila with a complement of about 30 Ki-44s, half of which were Ki-44-II Otsus. Whilst in Burma these aircraft had the 40 mm cannon removed from the wings, some weapons being replaced with 12.7 mm machine guns, but many of them flew with just their two 12.7 mm cowling weapons.

On the day of their arrival at the central Burmese airfields, the Ki-44s had been attacked by P-38s from the 459th FS, but none were reported lost. The Shokis were in furious action over Meiktila on 11 May when the P-51As of the 530th FS conducted a sweep over the airfield complex. The 87th fared badly in this combat, having 1Lt Hiroshi Hashimoto and Sgts Mitsuo Kobayashi, Kadoaki Nomachi and Hideo Kuriyama killed. Capt Hirobumi Nakamatsu, the 1st Chutai commander, was also shot down, although he managed to bail out. In turn, the 87th claimed three Mustangs shot down, although none were in fact lost.

The 530th FS returned to Meiktila the following day and engaged the 87th once again. This time the Japanese had WO Kiyomitsu Sato and Sgt Kadoaki Machino killed. The 87th claimed four Mustangs shot down. On 14 May 12 Ki-44s of the 87th, together with six 'Oscars' from the 64th Sentai, reported engaging 16 P-51s and ten P-38s over Meiktila. The 87th claimed five Mustangs shot down and two probables, but lost another two Ki-44s, with Sgt Tsuchiya bailing out.

Whilst in Burma the 87th participated in two offensive sweeps. On 15 and 18 May it joined 'Oscars' from the 50th and 64th Sentais in the escort of Ki-48 'Lily' bombers sent to attack airfields in the Hukawng area. On the 15th Lt Takao Mihara was returning to land at Heho when P-38s from the 459th FS attacked the airfield. He leapt from his aircraft as it was still rolling and managed to survive. On the 18th, the Japanese fighters clashed with RAF Spitfires of Nos 81 and 607 Sqns. The JAAF pilots claimed 12 shot down without loss, although only two Spitfires were actually lost. Flt Sgt W G Goodwin of No 607 Sqn was shot down and killed whilst Flg Off D H Hamblyn of No 81 Sqn bailed out.

The unit returned to Sumatra on 22 May. According to one Japanese report the 87th had not been able to utilise the full potential of its Ki-44s since it had no combat experience.

A Ki-44 of the 87th Sentai following a forced landing at an airfield in Japan. The unit's emblem represented the billowing "bag of wind" carried by the Shinto God of the Wind, Fūjin. The 87th were stationed at Kashiwa, Japan, from July to December 1943, before being transferred to the East Indies. Several of its aircraft that were deployed there continued to wear the white Homeland Defence recognition 'bandages' as seen on this Shoki (*Yasuho Izawa*)

PALEMBANG

On 16 January 1945 the British Pacific Fleet (BPF) began Operation *Meridian*, which saw its carrier-based aircraft targeting refineries and airfields in the Palembang area of southern Sumatra. The operation was conducted by four fleet aircraft carriers supported by one fast battleship, three light cruisers and nine destroyers. Avengers, Fireflies, Corsairs and Hellcats from the carriers *Illustrious, Indefatigable, Indomitable* and *Victorious* executed the attacks.

Eight days later a force of 133 aircraft attacked the refinery at Plaju and airfields at Lembak, Palembang and Talangbetoete, whilst on 29 January 124 aircraft targeted the airfields and refineries of Sungai Gerong. In addition, the coastal airfield at Mana was attacked on both days. The Japanese air defence, which included the 87th Sentai's Ki-44s and kamikaze suicide attacks against the BPF ships, was spirited, and the Fleet Air Arm (FAA) lost a total of 41 aircraft – 16 in combat and 11 ditching with damage received in combat.

One of the 87th's Ki-44 pilots, ace Hideaki Inayama, described his experiences flying against the FAA aircraft on 24 January. Inayama had been chatting to his crew chief prior to a routine day of flying and was chalking patrol assignments on the blackboard outside the dispersal hut when the airfield air raid siren suddenly started up and the dispersal alarm klaxon was sounded. Inayama shouted to the pilots in his flight to get airborne and ran to his own aircraft, which had been started up by his mechanic. He was already rolling down the runway when tracers began flashing past his starboard wing and two FAA Corsairs streaked past above him.

Flying in a shallow climb at 220 mph, Inayama glanced around wondering whether the rest of his flight had got off the ground safely. He could not see any of them, although he saw other Ki-44s climbing rapidly in the distance, and he resolved to press on alone. Inayama made a tight climbing turn to port, opened his throttle and headed for Palembang. Calling his base for instructions, he was told that more than 100 enemy aircraft had crossed the coast and were attacking the refinery area. At 12,000 ft Inayama switched on his oxygen and continued climbing. At 15,000 ft over the refineries, he saw 15 or 16 Ki-44s circling, and realised that the unit had already suffered losses in the Corsair strafing attack.

Inayama next spotted anti-aircraft fire erupting between layers of scattered cloud at 6000 ft – he also heard warning shouts in his headphones. Then he saw a formation of nine aircraft in vics of three, escorted by Corsairs and Hellcats. Inayama joined the other Ki-44s in the attack, diving straight down through the fighter escort and heading for the bombers that he identified as Avengers. Throttling back to reduce his excessive speed from the dive, he closed behind the starboard aircraft in the last vic and fired all his guns. The Avenger's bomb-bay doors were already open as Inayama fired. Overtaking the Avenger, he pulled up into a steep climbing turn and, glancing back, thought he saw it burst into flames and spin down into the jungle below.

The remaining Avengers were in a shallow dive dropping their bombs, and Inayama felt a surge of admiration for their determination despite the

Lt Hideaki Inayama of the 87th Sentai flew his Ki-44 against aircraft of the British Pacific Fleet at Palembang in early 1945. Lt Inayama survived the war with a score of at least five kills (*via Henry Sakaida*)

anti-aircraft barrage. He now seemed to be alone in the sky, but he fired a brief burst at an aircraft passing in front of him, before pulling up in another steep climb. A Hellcat flashed past his starboard side.

Inayama was now flying at 3000 ft, and he had been warned by radio that a second wave of enemy aircraft was approaching. His fuel state was low and he was anxiously looking for signs of other Japanese aircraft. Below him, Inayama spotted a Hellcat on the tail of a Ki-43 Hayabusa, and he half rolled and dived down on the two aircraft that were in a tight turn to port. He fired a brief burst as the Hellcat flashed through his gunsight and then turned in sharply to try to get behind it. Inayama overshot and found himself flying almost level with the Hellcat on its starboard side, glancing across to see a look of astonished surprise from its pilot. He pulled up, intending to try to loop onto the Hellcat's tail, but it dived away suddenly to starboard, beneath his aircraft, and made off close to the jungle canopy. The reprieved 'Oscar' pilot flung his aircraft into several high-spirited rolls to signal his gratitude to Inayama for his rescue.

Inayama climbed to 9000 ft in wide circles over the refineries, with their rising columns of heavy black smoke, and found his windscreen was partly obscured by oil. Some 3000 ft below him at his 'ten o'clock' he spotted two Ki-44s flying together, but as he dropped down to join them he saw the second wave of Avengers approaching from the south at about 6000 ft. At that moment the anti-aircraft fire again erupted over the refineries, and he saw an Avenger burst into flames and break up, a broken wing falling away.

Keeping an eye on the top cover of Hellcats that had broken into scattered flights, Inayama went straight for the Avengers, barrel rolling up beneath them, firing at the closest aircraft and climbing steeply through them. A flight of four Hellcats latched on to him almost immediately, and he pulled into a sharp turn to port, watching two of them overshoot. Pulling maximum g, but realising he could not hope to turn the Ki-44 inside the Hellcat, Inayama glanced anxiously over his shoulder to see a Grumman fighter 400 yards behind him and closing. He pulled the Shoki into another vertical turn to port as the Hellcat opened fire and the tracer flashed behind his tail.

Thinking he had only seconds to live, Inayama was saved when a sudden barrage of anti-aircraft fire blossomed between the two Hellcats, forcing them to break away in a starboard turn. Inayama pulled the nose of his Ki-44 up and began climbing once again.

The air battle now seemed over, and the Avengers, having dropped their bombs, were egressing the target area. Checking his fuel state, Inayama dived after two Avengers that he could see flying at 1500 ft, the leader trailing a ribbon of smoke. He concentrated first on the damaged Avenger that still had its bomb-bay doors open. Ignoring the return fire from its gun turret, and wrestling with the turbulence from the bomber's airflow, he closed to almost point blank range and opened fire with all four guns. The Avenger's long canopy shattered, flames licked back from the port wing root and it rolled inverted towards the jungle below.

Inayama now turned his attention towards the second Avenger, which also appeared to have been damaged – it had a large hole near its starboard wingtip and torn aluminium was flapping in the slipstream.

A view of the left side of the
Ki-44 cockpit, showing the throttle.
This was pulled back to open it
and pushed forward to close. The
lever on the front of the throttle,
controlled by the index and middle
fingers, is the trigger for the guns
(*Kikuchi Collection via Hiroshi
Umemoto*)

There was no return fire from the bomber, and he could not see a gunner in the turret. The Avenger was flying at 500 ft and Inayama resolved to finish it off. He throttled back and drew up alongside the stricken Avenger, staring over his port wing at the pilot struggling with his controls. Then, pushing the throttle forward, Inayama put his Ki-44 into a steep climb, intending to attack the Avenger in a diving turn. But before he could complete the manoeuvre his quarry had reached the safety of scattered cloud and disappeared.

With an alarmingly low fuel state, Inayama headed back to his airfield. When he returned, anxious groundcrew greeted him, and informed him that he was the only member of his chutai that had managed to get airborne to oppose the raids. The 87th had lost 12 Ki-44s and had had seven pilots killed or wounded that day. The unit was in turn credited with 15 victories and 13 probables, with three successes being claimed by Capt Yasutaka Ito, who force-landed with severe wounds. Pilots from the 87th claimed a further 14 victories on 29 January, although the sentai lost four pilots to FAA fighters.

Hideaki Inayama ended the war with claims for more than five aerial victories. Following service with the 87th he flew Kawasaki Ki-100 fighters with the 111th Sentai in the defence of Japan, commenting that Kawasaki's makeshift hybrid (a radial engine mated to the Ki-61 Hien 'Tony' airframe) had 'the best manoeuvrability of all the JAAF's frontline fighters with the exception of the Ki-43, which meant that pilots with only a little experience could both fly and fight it easily'. Inayama went on to serve postwar as a major in the Japanese Air Self-Defence Force (JASDF).

The Ki-44's control column was
topped by two buttons that were
the 'up' and 'down' controls for the
fighter's 'butterfly' flaps. These
could be quickly deployed during
combat in order to tighten a turn
(*Kikuchi Collection via Hiroshi
Umemoto*)

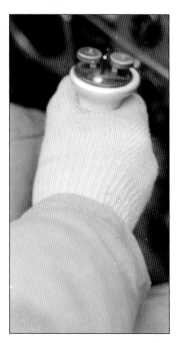

On 4 March the 87th moved from Gelumbang to a satellite airfield at Tandjung Paro, but it saw no further action. A strength report for 14 March indicated that the unit had been reduced to 17 Ki-44s. On 23 July the 87th moved to Singapore.

SINGAPORE

In Singapore, the unique 1st Yasen Hoju Hikotai (Field Reserve Air Unit) under 3rd Air Army command operated a full complement of JAAF types in four units equipped with fighters, light bombers, medium bombers and reconnaissance aircraft from Tengah airfield. The main purpose of the unit was to provide operational training for aircrew scheduled for assignment to units in the 3rd and 4th Air Armies. In addition to this role, the unit augmented the air defence capability of Singapore, evaluated aircraft tactics and weapons and employed captured enemy aircraft (including a B-17 Flying Fortress) to provide combat training.

When China-based B-29 Superfortresses began raiding Singapore on 5 November 1944, the ten Ki-44s of the unit were active in defence. One of the intercepting Shoki pilots was Capt Ryotaro Jobo, who would eventually have a total of 76 aerial victories attributed to him (although he personally claimed only 30) and gain the reputation of being a 'B-29 specialist'. He was reported to have destroyed or damaged as many as 12 B-29s in the CBI theatre. Against the Superfortresses over Singapore, Jobo flew Ki-44s fitted with experimental wing-mounted rocket launchers and Ta-dan air-to-air cluster bombs.

The first B-29 attack on Singapore was Mission No 15 on 5 November 1944, with 53 aircraft successfully reaching the primary target. B-29 42-6370 *Lethal Lady*, flown by 468th BG commander Col Ted Faulkner, was lost and its crew posted as missing in action. The second attack was Mission No 27 on 11 January 1945, when 32 bombers targeted Singapore's floating dry dock and King's dry dock, but no losses were reported. On 1 February the floating dry dock was again targeted by 78 B-29s in Mission No 33. This time two B-29s were lost, 42-24589 *Calamity Jane* being brought down by flak and 42-24736 crash-landing upon its return to base, the bomber's No 4 engine having been feathered as a result of combat damage. On 24 February the Empire dock was the target of 105 bombers, but only one was lost, 42-24479 ditching on the return flight. On 2 March 50 B-29s targeted Sembawang naval base in Mission No 41, and although no bombers were lost, several returned damaged from air interception.

The JAAF fighter opposition to these missions was rated as weak, although the attacks were coordinated with pairs of fighters. The crews estimated that almost half of the Japanese gunnery runs were broken off between 250 and 500 yards, with only a quarter being pressed home closer than 250 yards. Most of these were high and from the front quarter (the '12 O'clock Express', as the crews referred to it), with the Japanese fighters coming in high at 1000 yards and rolling inverted to begin firing at 500 yards in a diving pursuit curve, before passing within 25 yards of the B-29's tail.

During these interceptions there were 11 attempts to disrupt the formation with Ta-dan bombs – both phosphorous and fragmentation – but none of them damaged any of the Superfortresses. The closest bomb exploded 50 yards off the wingtip of a B-29, but most detonated 200-400 yards out from the formation. The air-to-air bombs were either dropped in level flight or 'flipped', being released as the fighter dived towards the formation and rolled away.

Jobo, a master swordsman and 28 years old when flying over Singapore, had served in the 64th Sentai during the Nomonhan fighting, claiming 18 Soviet fighters shot down prior to being wounded. He also served with the 33rd Sentai in the China theatre, where he claimed two additional P-40 kills. Ryotaro Jobo survived the war.

Capt Ryotaro Jobo was one of the highest scoring JAAF aces to fly the Ki-44. His final score of 30+ victories included B-29s claimed destroyed or damaged over Singapore whilst flying rocket-armed Ki-44s of the 1st Field Reserve Air Unit (*via Henry Sakaida*)

THE END IN CHINA

In January 1944 Imperial General Headquarters had approved the *Ichi-Go* ground offensive in China along the Hunan-Kwangsi, Canton-Hankow and Peiping-Hankow railway lines, with the express purpose of destroying the threat posed by US airfields in south-west China. One of the prime objectives of *Ichi-Go* was to 'forestall the bombing of the Japanese Homeland by American B-29s from bases in Kweilin and Liuchow'. The Japanese expected these 'super bombers' to begin combat operations in May or June.

In preparation for this offensive, the 3rd Air Division was redesignated as the 5th Air Army Headquarters, with the 1st Air Brigade – controlling two fighter regiments (including the Ki-44-equipped 85th Sentai) and two light bomber regiments – under its command. 5th Air Army Headquarters also controlled a direct support regiment, three independent squadrons of reconnaissance and close support aircraft and a training brigade that consisted of five units. 5th Air Army Headquarters estimated that the strength of these units in terms of both aircrew and aircraft was only between a third and a half of their authorised strength.

In addition, although an average of about 50 aircraft a month were being received into the theatre to replace losses and make up unit strengths, operational pilots from the frontline sentais were needed to ferry them from Japan. This ongoing requirement hindered training, as did a shortage of fuel. Indeed, the new Air Army estimated that it only had sufficient aviation fuel in China for about six months of operations. Therefore, additional supplies would be required to continue operations through to August.

The ratio of Japanese-to-Allied air strength in China at the beginning of the 1944 operations was 1-to-2, but by the time the *Ichi-Go* ground offensive was launched in May 1944 that ratio had dropped to 1-to-5.3. Japanese Air Staff officers noted that 'As veteran pilots were continually lost they were replaced by inexperienced men who had just completed basic training, so that the skill of the pilots dropped rapidly in quality. The supply of aeroplanes and parts from Japan proved inadequate, making it necessary to put back into service even obsolete aeroplanes that previously had been used as trainers in the rear'.

A novice Japanese pilot in the theatre complained that there were usually more pilots than aircraft, and that it was very difficult to acquire experience alongside the veteran aviators. Novice pilots chosen piecemeal to accompany more experienced flyers were vulnerable, and they often failed to return from missions. Once combat was initiated against greater odds, even the veteran pilots routinely had to abandon discipline and fly for themselves. Briefings on the ground constantly emphasised the need for air discipline, but the reality of combat was very different in an environment where the Japanese fighter pilots were usually outnumbered.

The 9th Sentai, under the command of Maj Tatsuo Takanishi, was another Ki-44-equipped unit that was transferred from Manchuria into

north China during February 1944 as part of the preparations for the *Ichi-Go* offensive. The 9th had transitioned to the Ki-44 at Akeno, in Japan, from May 1943, having converted directly from the Ki-27. It returned to Manchuria in September 1943. Ostensibly a well-trained unit, the 9th had little opportunity to gain valuable combat experience in the Ki-44 before being committed to the demanding pace of air operations in China. Nevertheless, the sentai would gain a reputation for being the most successful unit to combat the B-29s flying their first bombing missions from bases in China.

On 12 February the 85th participated in one of a series of attacks and sweeps against Suichuan, 11 Ki-44s flying top cover for 14 Ki-43s of the 11th Sentai. As the JAAF fighters approached Suichuan from Kanchow at about 20,000 ft, the Americans countered them with a force of P-40s, P-51As and P-38s. Although the Japanese had an altitude advantage on this occasion, they failed to exploit it. Capt Yukiyoshi Wakamatsu was in action, and he shot down the P-40 of Lt William Butler of the 76th FS, who was killed. The P-38 of Lt Art Masterson was also shot down, but he managed to bail out and return to Suichuan two days later. These were the only successes for the Japanese that day.

Wakamatsu's Ki-44 was seriously damaged in the fight, and he had to return to base prematurely, where he waited anxiously for his comrades. The Shokis had fared badly, and only two pilots returned to tell Wakamatsu that they had seen one Ki-44 shot down during the fight. Five 'Tojos' failed to return and three crash-landed after running out of fuel, one of them flown by Maj Togo Saito, the sentai commander. Five of the 85th's pilots had been killed in the battle – Lt Kiyona Kon-I, Sgt Maj Kenji Takahashi and Sgts Tadashi Kikukawa, Haruzo Hayakawa

Following the death of Capt Akira Horaguchi (see page 25 for details), pilots and groundcrew of the 85th Sentai's 1st Chutai conduct a dedication ceremony for their aircraft on New Year's Day 1944. The pilot standing in front of the propeller is Capt Horaguchi's successor, Lt Hajime Saito, who would be killed in action over Canton on 5 October 1944 (*Yasuho Izawa*) and Keiishi Kimura. The Japanese flyers claimed to have shot down five American fighters.

At the time of the *Ichi-go* offensive the 85th Sentai, still with its main force split between Hankow and Canton, had only eight officer pilots, albeit all rated 'A' in terms of experience and flying hours. There were only five warrant officers or NCO pilots of the same rating, with 13 more being rated 'B' and 20 in the least proficient category of 'C'. The unit had less than half the number of officer pilots required. Although the strength of warrant officer and NCO pilots was 95 percent of the total required, 86 percent of them were relatively inexperienced with low flying hours. At the same time the 85th's equipment strength was reported to be eight Ki-43s and 32 Ki-44s. Because the 'Tojo' was considered a handful to fly, the 'Oscars' were used to provide additional flying training for the less-experienced pilots.

On 9 March the 9th Sentai moved to Wuchang, in central China, to conduct interception missions with the 25th Sentai against the increasing number of B-24 and B-25 raids. Before getting the chance to engage the enemy, however, the 9th was urgently transferred to Anking, in Manchuria, for the Keikan operation. It returned to north China in April, leaving the 3rd Chutai behind in Anking.

Ki-44 production had peaked just before *Ichi-go* was launched, with 85 aircraft rolling off the production line in April 1944, and it would thereafter decline steadily to the end of the year. In March the final mass production armament version, the Ki-44-II Hei, which was fitted with four 12.7 mm Ho-103 machine guns (two in the cowling firing synchronised through the propeller and one in each wing), began replacing the Otsu. The proposed Ki-44-III versions that were intended to be armed with four 20 mm cannon or two 20 mm cannon paired with two 37 mm weapons would not go beyond a single prototype built in January 1945, and it would represent the end of the line for the Shoki.

The 9th was initially deployed to Hsinhsiang, in north China, to provide air defence for the strategic Pawangcheng Bridge across the Huang Ho River and to undertake combat air patrols (CAPs), with special emphasis on protecting the railway systems. It was reported that the unit only had around ten Ki-44s suitable for operations at this time, and its advance warning radar at Kaifeng was unserviceable. The unit was also under direct Army command during this period. The 9th's ranks were augmented by providing the unit with additional 'Oscars'. By May its strength had risen to 11 Ki-43s and 14 Ki-44s.

On 16 May a 9th Sentai CAP of three Ki-44s was bounced eight miles south-west of Luoyang by four P-40s of the 7th PFS of the 3rd FG CACW. These aircraft, led by Maj Bill Reed, were on a search mission to destroy a Warhawk that had force-landed behind Japanese lines. Reed claimed one Ki-44 destroyed and another one damaged, while Lt Wilbur Walton was credited with destroying a second 'Tojo'. Lt Tan Kun was shot down, but subsequently managed to return to

Maj Togo Saito, commander of the 85th Sentai, led the unit throughout the fighting over China, despite being wounded in the epic air battle over Hankow on 18 December 1944 (*Yasuho Izawa via Hiroshi Umemoto*)

Aircraft of the 9th Sentai photographed at Nanking, China, after the war. By this time the unit was flying a mixture of Ki-84s and Ki-44s, and at least six of the latter can be seen in this view (*Carl Molesworth*)

his unit. Sgt Shin-ichi Bando and Cpl Hikiyasu Ito of the 9th were shot down and killed.

The *Ichi-go* offensive finally began on 27 May, with substantial Japanese ground forces pushing south and south-west from the Tungting and Poyang lakes areas. Despite a concerted effort to stop the advance with air power, by late June Changsha had fallen to the Japanese. Hengyang fell on 10 August, Lingling was evacuated later that month and Kweilin had been abandoned by mid September. Finally, at the end of November Liuchow had to be evacuated too. By the end of 1944 the Japanese had accomplished their two primary objectives – the establishment of a land route between north China and French Indochina and the neutralisation of the US airfields along the Hunan-Kwangsi railway.

As part of the early stages of the *Ichi-go* offensive, on 2 June Capt Isao Kobayashi was patrolling with seven Ki-44s of the 9th's 3rd Chutai when they encountered a force of P-40s of the 7th and 8th (P)FSs of the CACW on a bombing mission over the Changtsien railway marshalling yards. Capt Omori, who was leading a vic of three Ki-44s at 6000 ft, first spotted the Warhawks some 2400 ft below him and 'bounced' them. 1Lt Yoshitaro Yoshioka, who would become a six-victory ace in China, attacked one of the P-40s, closing to 40 yards and hitting it. The fighter dived away trailing a plume of black smoke, this being the first of two Warhawk claims made by Yoshioka following this combat. Yoshioka's first victim was possibly Lt Chang C M of the 7th FS, who was reported missing in action. The 9th's pilots were credited with five P-40s shot down, whilst the CACW pilots claimed seven and two probables in return. Sgt Fumio Oguri, who was shot down and killed, was the sentai's sole loss, however.

On 11 June the 9th's detached chutai at Anking suffered at the hands of the 449th FS when 2Lts Jack V Frank and James E Nunn shot down and killed Capt Michio Iwata, the 1st Chutai leader, and Sgt Kazuyasu Kamidozono. The squadron's 12 Lightnings, which had been bounced whilst on a ground attack mission, also engaged Ki-43s from the 48th Sentai. Capt Eiji Yuzuki replaced Capt Iwata.

Two days later the 9th lost Sgt Kazuo Miyasaki to the guns of another 449th P-38 when he attempted to engage a formation of B-25s that were attacking Hankow.

On 18 June four Ki-44s from the unit joined 12 'Oscars' from the 25th Sentai in the interception of a small force of B-25s, escorted by 12 P-38s, over Anking. The 9th provided top cover whilst the Ki-43s attacked the Lightnings, shooting down two for no loss.

Exactly a week later, 1Lt Yoshitaro Yoshioka claimed two more P-40s and was pursuing a third when his engine failed and he had to make a deadstick landing – no mean feat in a Ki-44. He was flying one of seven Shokis from the 9th that had been led aloft by 3rd Chutai leader Capt Isao Kobayashi against a force of B-25s, escorted by P-40s of the 32nd FS CACW, attacking the Yellow River bridges. The 9th claimed three Warhawks destroyed and one probable, but on the same day lost TSgt Yoshiyori Kudo, Sgt Tadashi Ito and Cpl Hisakichi Yanagisawa, who were all killed in action when the 1st Chutai, under Capt Eiji Yuzuki, was bounced by a superior force of P-40s over Xinxiang. During

Yoshitaro Yoshioka was the 9th Sentai's leading ace in China, claiming six victories. He made two successful deadstick landings in the Ki-44 – an almost unheard of feat – but on the second occasion he was badly injured. Providing stalwart leadership to the unit after the commander and other senior officers had been killed, Yoshioka survived the war and remained in China to train local pilots to fly the Ki-84. Upon his return to Japan he joined the Japan Self-Defence Army and was promoted to the rank of lieutenant colonel (*Yasuho Izawa*)

these combats the CACW pilots were credited with six destroyed, one probable and one damaged. Despite the 3rd Chutai claims, it appears that no Warhawks were actually lost to the Ki-44s. One 'Tojo' attacked Maj Bill Turner in a head-on pass and another got within 50 yards of his tail, but he was not hit.

Two more 85th Sentai pilots fell to the guns of 118th Tactical Reconnaissance Squadron (TRS) Mustangs on 14 July when they were caught in a sweep over Tangchuk. 1Lt Tadashi Okano and Sgt Masanori Katayama might have been flying Ki-43 'Oscars' during this fight as no 'Tojos' were identified by the American pilots involved. Ten days later the 74th FS swept in on a 'school' of 'Oscars' and 'Tojos' doing 'circuits and bumps' at Siangton, south of Changsha, and quickly claimed four of the Ki-44s destroyed. The Shokis were 'low and slow', some with wheels and flaps down. One of them pulled up into a steep climb, but was caught at the top and shot down. During the fight Capt John 'Pappy' Herbst was providing top cover for the attacking force at 8000 ft when he saw three black-painted 'Tojos' approaching him. He turned into them and they immediately broke away, not being seen again.

Although the 74th's 'Tojo' opponents have since been identified as coming from the 9th Sentai, no 9th or 85th pilots were reported lost on 24 July.

MANCHURIAN INTERLUDE

On 29 July 1944 96 B-29s of XX Bomber Command conducted Mission No 4 against the Showa steelworks at Anshan, Manchuria – 60 Superfortresses reached and bombed the primary target. Japanese air opposition was limited to about 20 fighters hastily formed into a provisional defence unit, which included the 9th Sentai's detached chutai. Only five Ki-44s from the 9th sortied, the sentai's newly appointed commander, Maj Takehisa Yakuyama, leading the fighters aloft. The unit attacked 468th BG B-29 42-6274 *Lady Hamilton*, flown by Capt Robert Mills and his crew, which had already been damaged by flak. The Ki-44 pilots succeeded in shooting out the bomber's No 2 engine, forcing the crew to bail out. A month later eight survivors reached Chengtu after walking out through occupied China. Credit for this kill was given to Maj Yakuyama.

In response to the B-29 raid the Ki-44-equipped 70th Sentai was transferred from Japan to Manchuria, arriving at Anshan on 2 August 1944. In addition, the 104th Sentai, activated at Ozuki in Japan from elements of the 4th Sentai in July 1944, was transferred to Manchuria in September. The 104th was scheduled to be equipped with the new Nakajima Ki-84 Hayate (Gale) 'Frank' fighter, but delays in production resulted in the unit receiving interim equipment in the form of both the Ki-43 and Ki-44.

On 8 September the Shokis of the 9th and 70th Sentais were up to challenge Mission No 9 – a repeat attack against the Showa steelworks by 88 B-29s, of which 72 reached and bombed the primary target. The 9th claimed five bombers shot down on the way to the target and two probables and one damaged as the B-29s egressed. The 70th claimed three B-29s destroyed and six damaged, with one of the downed aircraft being credited to the unit's CO, Capt Atsuyuki Sakato, and another to

Yoshio Yoshida. The latter was destined to become a notable ace over Japan against the B-29 (see chapter six for details). Sgt Hideo Okumura of the 70th was shot down and killed by defensive fire from the bombers.

The USAAF recorded the loss of three Superfortresses, with 42-6234 of the 444th BG being the only one that was actually shot down. B-29 42-6360 of the 462nd BG belly landed at Lachokow with heavy combat damage, whilst 42-6212 from the same unit crashed three miles west of Hsian after running out of fuel.

On 26 September Mission No 10 saw 109 B-29s attack the Showa steelworks again, with 83 aircraft reaching and bombing the target. Although no B-29s were reported lost, 2Lt Okada claimed to have successfully attacked one of the bombers on its way to the target, and to have seen it drop out of its formation and go down trailing smoke. SSgt Kurotsuka claimed to have damaged another bomber.

After landing to refuel and re-arm their aircraft with Ta-dan air-to-air bombs, the 9th again intercepted the B-29s as they returned to their bases in China. 2Lt Okada claimed a second Superfortress destroyed and WO Akira Kawakita was credited with a victory too – he would ultimately down five B-29s over Manchuria in 1944. MSgt Mamoru Taguchi reported ramming one of the bombers, claiming to have hit its tailplane, but his Ki-44 was able to continue flying, and he landed safely.

In total, the 9th Sentai claimed five B-29s destroyed, two probables and eight damaged following the 26 September mission. The 70th and 104th were also up that day, and a probable claim was made by Capt Sakato of the former unit and 2Lt Nakamura from the latter sentai was credited with a B-29 destroyed. Another 70th pilot claimed a probable and several pilots reported damaging the bombers.

On 6 November 1944 the 70th Sentai returned to Japan, leaving the 104th Sentai in Manchuria. Early the following month the 104th was equipped with 28 Ki-44s, 12 Ki-84s and 11 Ki-43s.

The destructive potential of the Ki-44-II in combatting the B-29 was enhanced with the introduction of the Otsu variant on the production line during August 1944. This version of the fighter had the 12.7 mm machine guns moved to the cowling position to replace the 7.7 mm weapons, and it could also be armed with a single 40 mm Ho-301 cannon in each wing, with just ten rounds per gun, as special equipment. The Ho-301 was unusual in using caseless ammunition, where the propellant charge was contained within the lethal projectile itself.

Although previous references have disparaged this weapon, there is no doubt that against bomber aircraft it could be lethal, especially when used at night, where the attacking aircraft could approach much closer to its target before opening fire. The reason for disparagement is that the weapon had a low rate of fire (just 475 rounds per minute), a low velocity of about 804 ft per second and a limited range. Many Otsu variants were flown without wing armament, although some were retrofitted with 12.7 mm machine guns. Indeed, many units adopted this configuration for fighter-versus-fighter combat.

On 7 December 1944 XX Bomber Command's Mission No 19 targeted the Manchuria Aeroplane Company in Mukden, Manchuria, as the primary target for a force of 91 B-29s. The 104th Sentai countered the raid with 12 Ki-44s and six Ki-84s. 104th pilots Sgt Tadanori Nagata

Maj Yamato Takiyama was commander of the 104th Sentai when it briefly flew Ki-44s over Manchuria against the first B-29 raids on Anshan. Credited with a total of nine aerial victories, Takiyama participated in the claimed destruction of two B-29s in the Ki-44. He is seen here at an earlier point in his career posing in front of a Ki-27 (*Yasuho Izawa*)

and TSgt Yoshihiro Akeno had joined forces in the days leading up to this raid with the sole aim of ramming a B-29. They called their two-aircraft flight the Kikusui Tokutai (Floating Chrysanthemum Special Attack Unit).

The B-29 crews considered the Japanese defence of the aircraft factory to be aggressive, and the exceptionally clear conditions for bombing were offset by problems with frosting that created difficulties for bombardiers and turret gunners alike. Four B-29s were lost during the raid, although the Japanese defenders claimed 14, four via ramming attacks. Two bombers were indeed lost to ramming, USAAF crews reporting that three B-29s were hit in total, but in their opinion only one of them intentionally.

A Ki-45 'Nick' twin-engined fighter of the 25th Sentai, which had been badly shot up by gunners of the 468th BG's *Windy City II* and left with an engine on fire, pulled up under Capt Roger Parrish's *Gallopin' Goose* (42-6390) and rammed into the tail, tearing most of it away. Only one parachute was seen. Nagata of the 104th rammed B-29 42-6299 *Humpin' Honey* of the 462nd BG. There were no survivors. Akeno attempted to ram 468th BG B-29 42-63355 *Bella Bortion*, flown by Maj Douglas Hatfield, but struck the propeller of the bomber's No 1 engine instead and only succeeded in downing his own aircraft.

The 104th claimed a total of six victories, including B-29s shot down by the sentai's CO, Maj Yamato Takiyama, and by MSgt Narimoto, flying a Ki-44-II Otsu fitted with 40 mm wing cannon. The leader of the 104th's 2nd Chutai, 1Lt Mitsuo Tomiya, attempted to ram a third B-29 but was driven off by the bomber's defensive fire with serious damage to his Ki-44. Two other bombers failed to return from the mission. *Missouri Queen* (42-6359) of the 462nd BG went missing over the target, while the crew of *Marietta Misfit* (42-63363) of the 40th BG were forced to bail out of their seriously damaged B-29 on the return flight. *Old-Bitch-U-Airy Bess* (42-6273) of the 462nd BG was badly shot up, with one crewman being killed, by a fighter attack but it managed to return to base.

On 21 December XX Bomber Command returned to the Manchuria Aeroplane Company at Mukden with Mission No 23. A total of 40 Superfortresses bombed the target and only two losses were reported, although the Japanese fighter defence was described as 'vicious'. Capt John Campbell's *Wild Hair* (42-24505) was hit by a Ta-dan phosphorous bomb dropped by a fighter and the crew was seen to parachute out of the aircraft. Another B-29 (42-24715) of the 468th BG was rammed by a fighter and went straight down with one wing folded back. Maj Takiyama claimed another B-29 destroyed in this raid.

The 29-year-old Takiyama was a Nomonhan veteran with a distinguished record, flying as a flight leader in every one of his squadron's combats. On one occasion his Ki-27 was hit 44 times in a dogfight against 20 enemy aircraft, the fighter being so badly damaged that it turned over on landing. In 66 sorties Takiyama claimed six Soviet aircraft destroyed and five probables. Upon promotion to captain in March 1941 he was transferred to the 87th Sentai as a chutai commander. Takiyama subsequently attended the Army University, from where he graduated in 1944. His final victory tally was reported as nine, including two B-29s. He led the newly formed 104th Sentai from August 1944 through to May 1945.

CHINA FIGHTING INTENSIFIES

Whilst the Anking-based chutai was fighting B-29s, the rest of the 9th Sentai was active over north China, mainly challenging the operations of the CACW. For example, on 23 August six Ki-44s engaged eight P-40Ns of the 3rd FG that were escorting three B-25s of the 1st BG which had been sent to bomb a railway bridge west of Kaifeng. The Ki-44s hit the top cover and shot down Capt Tsang Si-lan, who crash-landed near Tungkwan. Capt Tsang claimed to have destroyed two Ki-44s before he was shot down, but no 'Tojos' were reported lost that day.

Two days later the 9th Sentai attempted to spring a trap on four Warhawks from the 32nd FS/3rd FG that were on a sweep of rail targets near Loyang. Formation leader Maj Bill Turner spotted four Ki-44s at 13,500 ft and climbed to engage them, the JAAF aircraft having by now commenced a mock dogfight amongst themselves so as to attract the Warhawks. The CACW flight continued to climb towards them, and they soon spotted a top cover of four more Ki-44s at 18,000 ft just waiting to pounce. Reaching the altitude of the top cover, the P-40s then dived on the first formation. Turner fired at a Ki-44 and reported that it rolled over smoking and then dove away, although he did not see it crash. Lt T C Liao claimed two more Ki-44s shot down.

Turner then pursued the low flight's leader and his wingman as they attempted to climb above the P-40s. He hit the wingman, closing to a mere 30 yards and seeing strikes on the Ki-44's cowling, cockpit and wings. The 'Tojo' caught fire and dived away, the pilot jettisoning the canopy but failing to bail out. The 9th reported that SSgt Takayuki Matsuhara had been killed in this engagement. At 18,000 ft a 'Tojo' from the top flight attacked Turner, but he too evaded by diving.

Meanwhile, Lts Liao and PC Tung had claimed another Ki-44 probably destroyed and one damaged. According to Turner, when the Warhawks returned to base at Hsian the pilots discovered that not one of them had been hit in the dogfight.

During July and August 1944 the 85th began transitioning to the new Ki-84 Hayate fighter, sending two pilots at a time to Hankow for this purpose. Wakamatsu himself, the arch exponent of the Ki-44, was impressed by the new fighter. 'Maximum speed, zoom and take-off run – everything is better than the Type 2 [Ki-44], and radio equipment is much improved'. Nevertheless, even after the unit was equipped with the Ki-84 he still had a Ki-44 maintained for his own use, and flew it on several missions thereafter.

Despite the promise of the sparkling new fighter, the odds against the JAAF in China were beginning to tell. By August 1944 the 85th Sentai had only five officer and five WO/NCO pilots rated 'A', with 20 WO/NCO pilots rated 'B' and nine WO/NCO pilots rated 'C'. The officer contingent of the sentai had dropped to 29 percent of strength, meaning that the 9th Sentai had only six officer pilots against its authorised strength of 13, five rated at 'A' and one rated at 'B'. Whilst the 9th fielded all 30 of its authorised WO/NCO pilots, only six were rated at 'A', four rated at 'B' and 20 rated at 'C'.

The decline in the fighter strength of the 5th Air Army during operations prior to the capture of Hengyang was significant. In addition, the commencement of the B-29 bombing campaign against Japan and Manchuria from bases in China made it essential that local JAAF strength was built up in order to cope. To achieve this Imperial General Headquarters temporarily assigned two more fighter units to the China theatre at the end of August 1944.

The 22nd Sentai arrived in-theatre equipped with the first examples of the Ki-84 'Frank' fighter. The 29th was another Ki-44-equipped sentai that moved to China from Formosa (Taiwan) on 24 August with around 20 fighters as a temporary reinforcement. Originally a reconnaissance unit, it had hastily converted to fighters in February 1944 in response to the expected B-29 operations. The 29th joined the 1st Air Brigade (Hiko Dan) at Wuchang, but sent detachments to operate from Erh Tao Kow, near Kiukiang, and from Pailochi, south of Hankow.

At that time the authorised strength of the 29th was 13 officer pilots, but the sentai could only field five, all 'A' rated. Against an authorised WO/NCO strength of 30, only 15 pilots were fielded, five rated 'A' and ten rated 'B'.

The unit was tasked with the air defence of the Hunan-Kwangsi area and to provide protection to bomber units cooperating with ground forces. Whilst in China the 29th had retained a base detachment flight of four Ki-44s on Formosa that were active in flying defence missions against the increasing number of US raids on the island. The 29th had been scheduled to remain in China for only one month, and as the raids on Formosa intensified the bulk of the unit returned to the island on 18 October 1944.

On 21 September 1944 a flight of eight 9th Sentai Ki-44s bounced six P-40s on a sweep north of Sinshih, but they did not spot the top cover of four more Warhawks above. The top cover P-40s dived on the Shokis, whose pilots spotted their attackers and dropped their belly tanks. The Warhawk pilots claimed two 'Tojos' destroyed and three damaged, but no 9th Sentai pilots were reported killed that day.

At the end of September the 85th Sentai received the first six examples of the Ki-84 to be allocated to the unit, and it would begin flying combat sorties in the new fighter from 4 October, whilst still using the Ki-44 as its primary equipment. On that day Wakamatsu led a mixed force of four Ki-84s and four Ki-44s into combat against Mustangs over Wuchow. Wakamatsu claimed one P-51 shot down, whilst his wingmen Sgt Maj Ohkubo and TSgt Ishikawa also claimed a Mustang each. The downed P-51s were flown by Capt Marks, who survived, and by Lts Rex Shull and Henry Leisses, both of whom were killed in action.

The following day six Ki-84s and 11 Ki-44s from the unit engaged Mustangs of the 118th TRS over Sanshui, on the outskirts of Canton, and lost 1st Chutai leader Lt Hajime Saito in a Ki-84 and Sgt Maj Toshiji Shoji and SSgt Nishimori in Ki-44s. Another Shoki had to be force-landed due to battle damage. USAAF pilots claimed three 'Tojos' destroyed and three probables, with these victories making one of the claimants, 1Lt Oran Stanley Watts, the first ace of the 118th TRS. The Ki-44 pilots were credited with four P-51s destroyed and one probable, plus a B-25 destroyed and one probable. The only USAAF loss, however, was Lt Jack Gocke of the 118th, who bailed out and later returned safely. Wakamatsu did not participate in this engagement as his Hayate had suffered mechanical problems.

85th Sentai commander Maj Saito flew a distinctively marked Ki-44 with a cobalt blue arrow emblem on the tail and broad blue fuselage band, the aircraft being seen here at Canton. Although not apparent in this view, the fighter is camouflaged in green and brown but the strong sun, high humidity and heavy rains in south China have taken their toll of the paintwork (*Yasuho Izawa via Hiroshi Umemoto*)

Three days later five Ki-44s from the 29th Sentai intercepted four Warhawks of the 74th FS that were attacking shipping between Pengtseh and Kiukang, west of Hukow. The 'Tojos' went for two P-40s 'down on the deck', and they were in turn attacked by two top cover fighters. The USAAF pilots claimed an 'Oscar' [sic] destroyed, with a probable and two damaged. In fact Sgts Mitsuo Hashimoto and Masao Gomi of the 29th were both reported killed. The fight was not entirely one-sided, however. One of the Ki-44s chased 1Lt Nick Gazibara more than 100 miles 'on the deck', hitting the Warhawk 12 times and shooting out its hydraulic system. The pursuit was so low that Gazibara even hit a tree, damaging his wing, before belly landing at Kian. The fighter had to be written off.

An element of the 85th Sentai staged to Formosa at about this time to assist in air defence against carrier strikes on the island. On 13 October WO Hajime Wakabayashi and Sgts Tsuneich Ishikawa and Koji Hikosaka were killed in action by US Navy Hellcats from the carrier task force.

More Ki-44s went down to the guns of P-51s on 15 October during the interception of a B-24 raid on Canton that was escorted by fighters from the 23rd FG. Sgt Maj Hiroji Shimoda and Sgt Tatsuji Uebo of the 85th Sentai were reported killed in action. The P-51 pilots claimed four 'Tojos' destroyed and two damaged in the fight, although Lt Jerome F Eisenman of the 76th FS was shot down – he returned to his unit in late

Another view of Maj Saito's distinctively marked Ki-44 of the 85th Sentai, as groundcrew prepare to chock the wheels following a sortie. The wear to the aircraft's camouflage paintwork is typical for this theatre (*Yasuho Izawa*)

November. WO Akiyoshi Nomura, flying one of the new Ki-84s, claimed two P-51s shot down, but his own aircraft was hit during the battle and the port wing fuel tank caught fire. Nomura was able to bail out without injuries. On the ground local Chinese residents came to his rescue, and he was returned safely to his unit by the evening of 17 October.

On 26 October WO Akira Kawakita, one of the leading aces of the 9th Sentai and a noted B-29 killer, fell victim to Mustangs of the 529th FS/311th FG between Wuchih and Kotangtien. Sgt Mitsuto Matsuo was also killed in this clash, the American pilots accurately claiming two 'Tojos' destroyed and two damaged.

At the beginning of November the 9th was still at Hsinhsiang, but it now came under the command of the 8th Air Brigade. It had a three-fold mission to engage in decisive air battles, to protect vessels on the Yangtze River from Hsiaochikou to the vicinity of Hankow and to provide air defence for the Wuhan area. With the 9th's limited air assets of only five serviceable Ki-44s flown by inexperienced pilots, this was an unrealistic expectation. In the middle of the month the sentai was reassigned to the 2nd Air Brigade and transferred to Canton, whilst the 85th, with 17 Shokis and ten Hayates, moved under the command of the 1st Air Brigade in place of the 9th.

On 16 November WO Akiyoshi Nomura of the 85th claimed another P-51 over Zhaoqing. Two Mustangs of the 26th FS, flown by Lts Pascoli and Duffy, had departed Nanning at 1050 hrs for an offensive reconnaissance of the Tanchuk-Ping and Nam-Wuchow areas. After bombing and sinking a 70 ft steamer, the Mustangs were bounced by Nomura and five other Ki-44s. Duffy's aircraft was hit and damaged in the first pass, but he managed to dive away and outrun the 'Tojos'. He saw one of the fighters then make a direct overhead pass on Pascoli, after which black smoke poured from the P-51. Although Pascoli failed to

Looking remarkably like a scale model, this Shoki of the 9th Sentai sits abandoned on an airfield in China. The captured Ki-44s and Ki-84s of the 9th were repainted in Nationalist Chinese markings, but it is doubtful that they saw much service with their new owners (*Campbell Archives/OKC*)

return from the mission, and his Mustang was lost, he possibly survived this encounter.

Raids against Hankow were increasing in their ferocity, and on 18 December it was targeted by Superfortresses. In Mission No 21 for XX Bomber Command, a total of 85 B-29s struck the primary target, followed by waves of B-24s and B-25s. It was a knockout blow on the airfield, with the 85th suffering grievous losses. Two of the unit's greatest aces, Wakamatsu and Shibata, were killed in the fighting and the sentai commander, Maj Togo Saito, was wounded. Sgt Maj Misao Ohkubo claimed a Mustang shot down (possibly from the 311th FG) whilst trying to defend Hankow, but he was then attacked by two more P-51s and wounded. Ohkubo managed to force-land his damaged Ki-44, but was hospitalised until May 1945. WO Akiyoshi Nomura was the only 85th pilot in the air that day not to be killed or wounded.

The damage to the sentai's fighting capability was immense, with only two or three serviceable aircraft surviving the attacks and ferocious air combat. The 85th Sentai was virtually finished as a fighter unit in China, although over the next four weeks enough Shokis were returned to service to allow the survivors of the unit to continue to fly interception missions over the Hankow area.

On 14 January 1945 29 fighters of the 5th FG, including 16 P-51s of the 75th FS (which was under CACW control), escorted B-24s to Hankow. Two Ki-44s attempted to climb up under the bombers but they were attacked by Capt Phil Coleman of the 26th FS. The Shoki leader turned into him head on and flashed past, with neither aircraft having time to fire, but Coleman then caught the wingman as he attempted to turn away in the other direction. He fired a two-second burst and the Japanese fighter caught fire, rolled over and dropped into the Yangtze River.

The 85th's last combat fatality over the Wuchang area occurred three days later when the 1st Chutai commander, Capt Nobuyuki Hironaka, was shot down and killed. His victor was possibly Capt Thomas D Harrison of the 92nd FS/81st FG, flying a P-47 Thunderbolt.

From July 1943 to December 1944 the 85th Sentai had had 25 pilots killed in aerial combat, this number representing 41 percent and 45 percent of its officer and WO/NCO complement, respectively, with several more pilots wounded and invalided home. Amongst the officers lost were seven experienced chutai commanders.

Towards the end of January 1945 the 85th Sentai was sent to Nanking to rest and refit. On 21 January Maj Thomas A Reynolds of the 7th (P)FS CACW caught a Ki-44 in the landing pattern over Nanking with its wheels extended, and he shot it down onto the airfield. The identity of the pilot, and whether he survived this crash, is unknown. The unit suffered two more fatalities whilst at Nanking.

Sgt Maj Misao Ohkubo (wearing the parachute) of the 85th Sentai stands in front of his Ki-44 with his groundcrew on New Year's Day 1944. The aircraft's spinner has been decorated for a dedication ceremony. Sgt Maj Ohkubo flew with Wakamatsu's 2nd Chutai, claiming a total of eight victories over China (*Yasuho Izawa*)

In May the 85th was moved to Tsinan, in north China, and after a few days here it was pulled out altogether to Kimpo, Korea, where it would remain until the end of the war. The glory days of the Ki-44 in China were almost over.

The 9th Sentai continued to fight in China, but with steady attrition of its remaining experienced pilots the unit experienced its own disastrous day over the Tien Ho and White Cloud airfields at Canton on 27 December 1944. No fewer than five pilots were killed, namely Maj Takehisa Yakuyama (sentai commander), Capt Eiji Yuzuki (1st Chutai leader), Sgt Maj Tokusaburo Nakagawa, Sgt Katsuji Kato and Cpl Kuniji Torizuka. Two more Ki-44s were shot down, with the pilots bailing out. The victories were claimed by the Mustangs of the 74th FS and 118th TRS.

On 15 January 1945 the 9th was in action against US carrier-based aircraft conducting strikes along the South China coast. Twenty Hellcats of VF-11, led by squadron CO Lt Cdr Gene Fairfax, were conducting a sweep along the coast between Hong Kong and Canton when they ran into the 9th's Ki-44s. Capt Isao Kobayashi (3rd Chutai leader) was shot down and killed and MSgt Mamoru Taguchi wounded. The next day the sentai was again in action with VF-11 and other squadrons from Vice Admiral John S McCain's Task Force (TF) 38 over Hong Kong. The US Navy flyers claimed a total of 13 Japanese aircraft shot down, although the 9th Sentai reported no losses. No fewer than 22 carrier aircraft were lost to all causes over Hong Kong, with most of these falling victim to flak that was described by the pilots as 'intense to incredible' – the most vicious they had yet seen. Two F6F pilots were amongst those killed by the flak, whilst a third bailed out just before his crippled Hellcat broke in two.

In March 1945 the 9th Sentai moved to Nanyuan, near Peking, and finally to Nanking. The unit's most notable flyer during its time with the Ki-44 was 1Lt Yoshitaro Yoshioka, a six-victory ace who had the dubious distinction of having to twice force-land Shokis without power – a notoriously difficult feat. On the second occasion, on 22 July 1944, he was badly injured. After the death of Maj Yakuyama on 27 December, Yoshioka effectively kept the unit together by dint of the fact that he was the 9th's best pilot. Surviving the war, he remained in China for a time, training local pilots to fly the Ki-84.

WO Rikio Shibata was one of the two top-scoring 85th Sentai Ki-44 aces in China, having previously claimed 14 (of his 27) victories flying the Ki-27 against the Soviets over Nomonhan in 1939 whilst serving in the 11th Sentai. He was killed in action over Hankow on 18 December 1944 (*Yasuho Izawa*)

Captured Ki-44s of the 9th Sentai briefly served with the Nationalist Chinese (Kuomintang) air force alongside other ex-Japanese aircraft within the 6th Fighter Bomber Group. 9th Sentai ace Yoshitaro Yoshioka trained Chinese student pilots to fly the Ki-84, but there is little evidence to prove that they were indeed used in combat during the civil war (*via C W Lam*)

THE PHILIPPINES

American troops landed on Leyte to begin the liberation of the Philippines on 17 October 1944. Japanese air reinforcements were rushed to the theatre almost immediately, and on 20 October the main force of the 29th Sentai, under the command of Capt Masatsugu Tsuchihashi, departed Hsiaochiang, on Formosa, for Clark Field, on Luzon, arriving with a complement of approximately 30 Ki-44s. Two days later the 246th Sentai departed Japan for Formosa in response to carrier task force raids against the island on 12 October that were expected to precede an invasion. When this failed to materialise, the 264th was also sent to the Philippines, arriving at Clark Field in early November. Throughout this period a base unit of the 246th remained at Taisho, in Japan, equipped with the Ki-44.

A camouflaged Ki-44 of the 246th Sentai abandoned in the Philippines. The sentai insignia – a stylised diving swallow on a red disk – was known as 'umeboshi', meaning a pickled red plum. This aircraft has racks for bombs beneath the wings. Note the Ki-45 'Nick' in the background (*Picarella Collection*)

This is the same aircraft as seen above, although this time from the front, showing the unusual – but not unique – spiral decoration on the spinner. Although usually representing the last two or three digits of the aircraft's serial number, the '338' on the undercarriage fairing of this machine has not been positively linked to a specific Ki-44 (*Picarella Collection*)

Officers of the 29th Sentai photographed at Sunjia, Manchuria, in May 1944. The Sentai commander, Maj Takeo Kawada, is the officer seated sixth from the left in the front row. The 29th began to equip with the Ki-44 from February 1944, and it flew the Shoki in Formosa, China and the Philippines, before re-equipping with the Ki-84 Hayate (*Yasuho Izawa*)

A Ki-44 of the 29th Sentai abandoned in the Philippines. This aircraft was painted in the late-war factory finish of olive brown, and it bears no discernable sentai insignia. The single character 'Mo' on the tail possibly represents the first syllable of the pilot's surname (*Picarella Collection*)

The mission for both the 29th and 246th was to provide CAP over Manila and escorts for 'special attack' (kamikaze) units staging through airfields in the area. The latter boasted a warren of dispersal taxiways and revetments, some of which were as far as 35 miles from the main runways.

Within days of their arrival the units were in action. On 13 November they were up from Clark Field to challenge a huge sweep by carrier task force fighters, mainly Hellcats, attacking shipping and installations in and around Manila Bay, including the Japanese airfields in the vicinity.

The same aircraft seen from the front, revealing the drop tanks carried inboard of the undercarriage. The Japanese character 'ki' (wood) is stencilled onto the front of each tank to indicate their plywood construction. Again, another Ki-45 can be seen in the background (*Picarella Collection*)

In the air battle over Clark Field the 29th lost four pilots, including the 3rd Chutai leader, Lt Tokuji Chiji-Iwa. The Japanese claimed nine victories and two probables whilst the US Navy admitted the loss of eight Hellcats, five Avengers and six Helldivers, many of them to ground fire. In official communiqués the task force claimed 18 of 20 intercepting

An apparently unarmed Ki-44 displaying the late-war factory camouflage of 'ohryoku nana go shoku' (yellow-green No 7 colour), which was an olive brown paint similar to US olive drab. Factories were instructed to apply this camouflage from June 1944. The undersurface of the aircraft was painted light brownish-grey, but there is evidence that many Ki-44s remained unpainted underneath. The cartouche on the rear fuselage is an advisory marking about the camouflage paint (*Robert C Mikesh*)

The cockpit of 'Tojo' serial number 2143, which was captured at Clark Field. This aircraft was a Ki-44-II Hei manufactured in October 1944 and, in compliance with the June 1944 instructions, the interior was probably painted in the same olive brown colour as the exterior. The butts of the cowling machine guns can be seen protruding into the cockpit on either side of the instrument panel. The reflector gunsight is the Army Type 100. Note the single lap belt used to secure the control column and the discarded parachute harness on the seat (*Robert C Mikesh*)

Japanese fighters shot down by Hellcats and ten downed by anti-aircraft fire as they approached the carriers.

During November the 1st Chutai of the 29th Sentai, under Lt Fumihiro Yabuta, was detached to serve with the 246th at Zablan (Manila East airfield). In addition, groups of the 29th's pilots were sent to Porac airfield, south of Clark Field, to undertake conversion training on the Ki-84 Hayate.

On 19 November seven Ki-44s from the 29th Sentai intercepted another strike force heading for the Manila area. Four pilots were shot down and killed, including Lt Yabuta. Six days later the unit lost three more pilots killed in action in an engagement over Manila. The 29th Sentai commander, Maj Masatsugu Tsuchihashi, perished on 7 December over Leyte together with four of his pilots, including sentai staff officer Capt Ryusuke Kinugasa. Following this rout the surviving

This abandoned 29th Sentai Ki-44, surrounded by other wrecked JAAF aircraft at an airfield in the Philippines, displays the unit's 'wave arrow' insignia that was long thought to be fictional. The 29th suffered badly in the Islands, losing 15 pilots in three combats between 15 November and 7 December 1944. The unit flew a mix of Ki-44s and Ki-84s during the campaign (*via James F Lansdale*)

An American serviceman examines an abandoned Ki-44-II Hei in the Philippines – possibly the same 29th Sentai aircraft seen above. The removable panel in front of the windscreen provided access to the cowling guns, facilitated also by the drop down doors on either side of the cockpit that were primarily for emergency escape if the aircraft should turn over. Beneath the removed cowling panel is the access panel for the ammunition box. The paint wear on the airframe is typical for the Ki-44 (*via James F Lansdale*)

The 40 mm Ho-301 wing cannon armament of abandoned Ki-44-II Otsu serial number 1747 is seen here in close up. This photograph was taken at Clark Field, Manila, by an ATAIU team sent to inspect the fighter. This particular Shoki was manufactured during March 1944 and probably issued to either the 29th or 246th Sentais (*Picarella Collection*)

pilots participated in the ground fighting around Mindanao until withdrawn from the area.

During the ill-fated defence of the Philippines special transport flights were established by the Hitachi Training Air Division to ferry replacement aircraft to the 29th and 246th Sentais from Japan via Formosa. The pilots, drawn from the division's instructors' pool, were led by Maj Yoshio Hirose, the 1st Hikotai leader. Spare parts and

Removed from a Ki-44-II Otsu, this 40 mm cannon has been photographed in uncocked or fired condition. On being cocked, the whole exterior frame forward of the receiver was drawn back to expose the barrel, the tip of which can be seen here. The Ho-301 fired unique caseless ammunition from a ten-round box magazine. During the defence of the Homeland 40 mm cannon-armed Ki-44s were sometimes flown in coordinated attacks with air-to-air ramming aircraft (*Picarella Collection*)

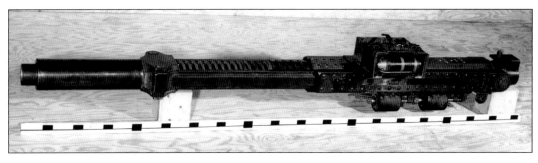

A Ho-301 40 mm round showing the perforated holes in the base of the projectile that allowed the charge to propel it, thus eliminating the need for loose cartridge cases to be ejected from the cannon. Primarily an anti-bomber weapon, the low muzzle velocity of the Ho-301 required the Ki-44 to approach close to its target – a near-suicidal tactic in daylight. The weapon was duly found to be most effective in nocturnal interceptions. In fighter-versus-fighter combat, the Ho-301 was often removed or replaced by the 12.7 mm Ho-103 machine gun (*Picarella Collection*)

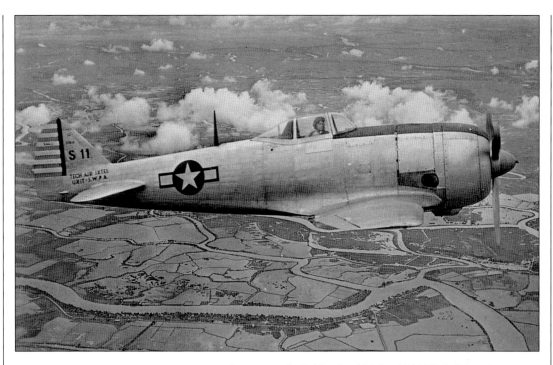

Found abandoned in the Philippines virtually intact, this Ki-44-II Hei was restored to flying condition and extensively evaluated by ATAIU pilots in mock combat with Allied fighter types (*Robert C Mikesh*)

groundcrew were ferried in aboard Mitsubishi Ki-57 'Topsy' transport aircraft operated by the 10th Flying Training Unit. These unarmed machines made at least 12 flights and lost five of the 11 aircraft committed to the operation.

On 14 December ten Ki-44s of the 246th were landing back at Zablan after a long-range escort of 'special attackers' to Silay when they were caught at low altitude with minimal fuel by another Hellcat sweep. The sentai commander, Maj Kanshi Ishikawa, immediately ordered the aircraft to force-land. Two pilots were lost and most of the Shokis were destroyed or damaged in the encounter. The previous day, four of the 246th's Ki-44s had scrambled to intercept P-38s over Silay, only for two of the Shokis to be shot down. Despite being at a tactical disadvantage when the Lightnings dived on them from above, the JAAF fighters split into two pairs and climbed head-on at the attacking P-38s. One of the aircraft subsequently lost was flown by flight leader WO Shozo Kawamoto, who was killed. On 26 December the survivors of the 246th returned to Japan for re-equipment (see chapter six for further details).

The handful of survivors from the 29th Sentai left the Philippines on 21 January 1945 to return to Formosa, where they remained until mid-February, re-equipping at Taoyuan. The unit then moved to Taichu-South, Taichung and Toen, all on Formosa, for re-equipment with Ki-84s. By 26 March it reported 25 Ki-84s and 13 Ki-44s on strength. At the end of March the unit was alerted for participation in Operation *Ten* (Sky), establishing the 'Sei Makoto' 33rd, 34th and 35th Special Attack Air Units during April from a core of 29th Sentai volunteers. During May and early June these units flew 43 'special attack' missions against Allied naval units around Okinawa and the southern Ryukyu Islands. On 6 June 1945 the 29th reported 37 Ki-84s (and no Ki-44s) on strength at Taichu-South, where it remained until war's end.

53

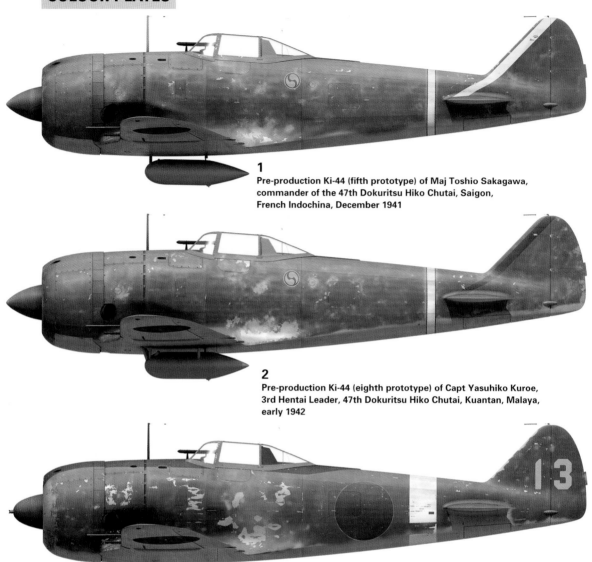

1
Pre-production Ki-44 (fifth prototype) of Maj Toshio Sakagawa,
commander of the 47th Dokuritsu Hiko Chutai, Saigon,
French Indochina, December 1941

2
Pre-production Ki-44 (eighth prototype) of Capt Yasuhiko Kuroe,
3rd Hentai Leader, 47th Dokuritsu Hiko Chutai, Kuantan, Malaya,
early 1942

3
Production series Ki-44-I of the 47th Dokuritsu Hiko Chutai, Mudon airfield, Moulmein, Burma, early 1942

4
Ki-44-I of the 33rd Sentai, Canton, China, early 1943

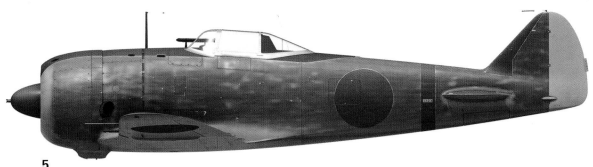

5
Ki-44-II Ko of Capt Yukiyoshi Wakamatsu, 2nd Chutai leader, 85th Sentai, Hankow, China, summer 1943

6
Ki-44-II Ko of Capt Yukiyoshi Wakamatsu, 2nd Chutai Leader, 85th Sentai, Tien Ho airfield, Canton, China, summer 1943

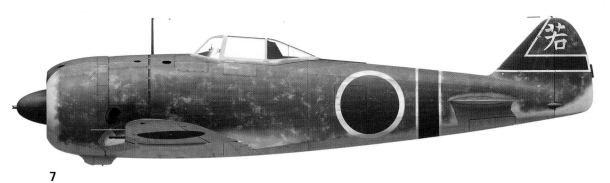

7
Ki-44-II Hei of Capt Yukiyoshi Wakamatsu, 2nd Chutai Leader, 85th Sentai, Canton, China, summer 1944

8
Ki-44-II Ko of 2nd Chutai, 85th Sentai, Hankow, China, summer 1943

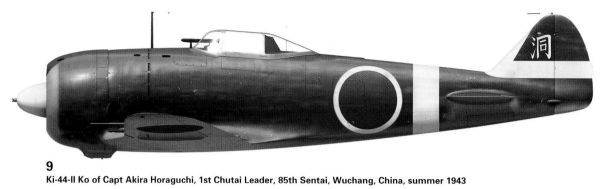

9
Ki-44-II Ko of Capt Akira Horaguchi, 1st Chutai Leader, 85th Sentai, Wuchang, China, summer 1943

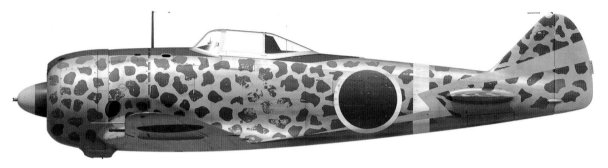

10
Ki-44-II Hei of the 50th Sentai, Meiktila, Burma, 1944

11
Ki-44-II Ko of Lt Shiro Suzuki, 4th Chutai, 64th Sentai, Rangoon, Burma, late 1943

12
Ki-44-II Otsu of the 87th Sentai, Meiktila, Burma, May 1944

13
Ki-44-II Hei of Lt Hideaki Inayama, 87th Sentai, Gloembang, Sumatra, January 1945

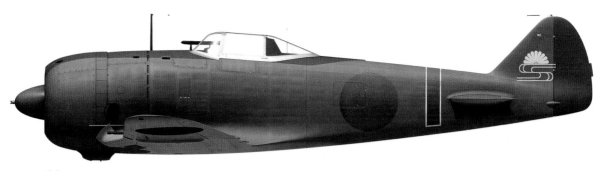

14
Ki-44-II Ko of Sgt Tadashi Kikukawa, 85th Sentai, Canton, China, late 1943

15
Ki-44-II Otsu of the 1st Chutai, 23rd Sentai, Imba, Japan, 1945

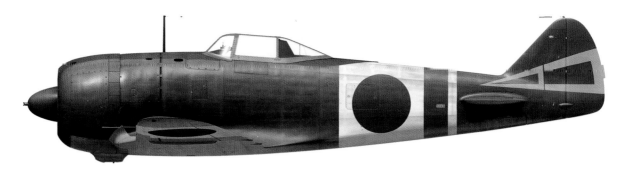

16
Ki-44-II Otsu of the 3rd Chutai, 70th Sentai, Anshan, Manchuria, August 1944

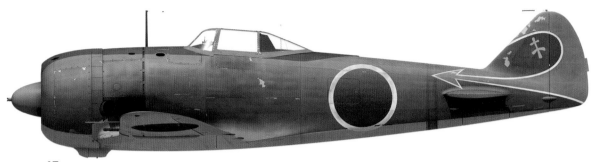

17
Ki-44-II Hei of the Sentai Hombu, 29th Sentai, Clark Field, the Philippines, November 1944

18
Ki-44-II Hei of the 29th Sentai, Hsiaochiang, Formosa, August 1944

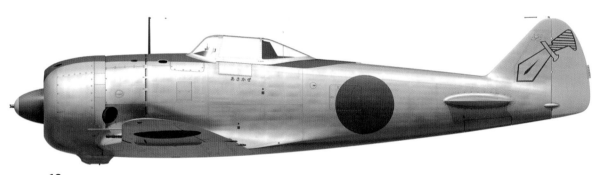

19
Ki-44-II Hei 'Asakaze' of the 2nd Chutai, 104th Sentai, Mukden, Manchuria, autumn 1944

20
Ki-44-I of the 47th Dokuritsu Hiko Chutai, Kashiwa, Japan, late 1942

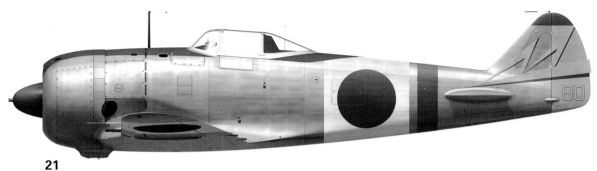

21
Ki-44-II Hei of Capt Teiichi Hitano, 3rd Chutai/Hikotai and 'Sakura' Leader, 47th Sentai, Narimasu, Japan, early 1944

22
Ki-44-II Otsu of MSgt Isamu Sakamoto of Shinten Seikutai, 47th Sentai, Narimasu, Japan, late 1944

23
Ki-44-II Otsu of Capt Jun Shimizu, 1st Chutai, 47th Sentai, Narimasu, Japan, 1944

24
Ki-44-II Hei of Capt Yasuro Mazaki, 2nd Chutai, 47th Sentai, Narimasu, Japan, late 1944

25
Ki-44-II Hei of the 246th Sentai, Clark Field, the Philippines, late 1944

26
Ki-44-II Hei of the 246th Sentai, Taisho, Japan, winter 1944-45

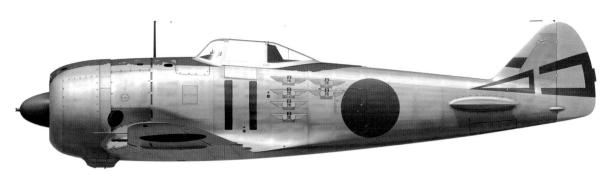

27
Ki-44-II Hei of Capt Yoshio Yoshida, 70th Sentai, Kashiwa, Japan, 1945

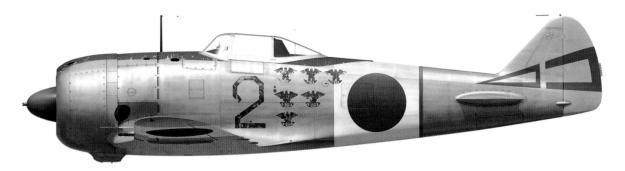

28
Ki-44-II Hei of WO Makoto Ogawa, 70th Sentai, Kashiwa, Japan, 1945

29
Ki-44-II Hei of the 3rd Chutai, 9th Sentai, Anking, China 1944

30
Ki-44-I of the Akeno Army Flying School, Japan, 1943

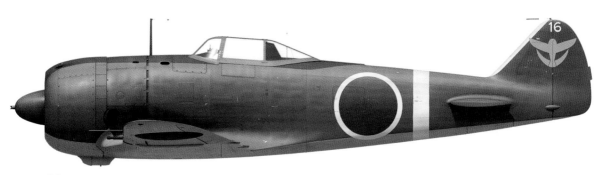

31
Ki-44-II Hei of Capt Ryotaro Jobo, 1st Field Reserve Air Unit, Singapore, 1944

32
Ki-44-II Hei of Maj Yoshio Hirose, 1st Hikotai of Hitachi TAD, Mito, Japan, December 1944

21 (above and right)
Ki-44-II Hei of Capt Teiichi Hitano, 3rd Chutai/Hikotai and 'Sakura' Leader, 47th Sentai, Narimasu, Japan, early 1944

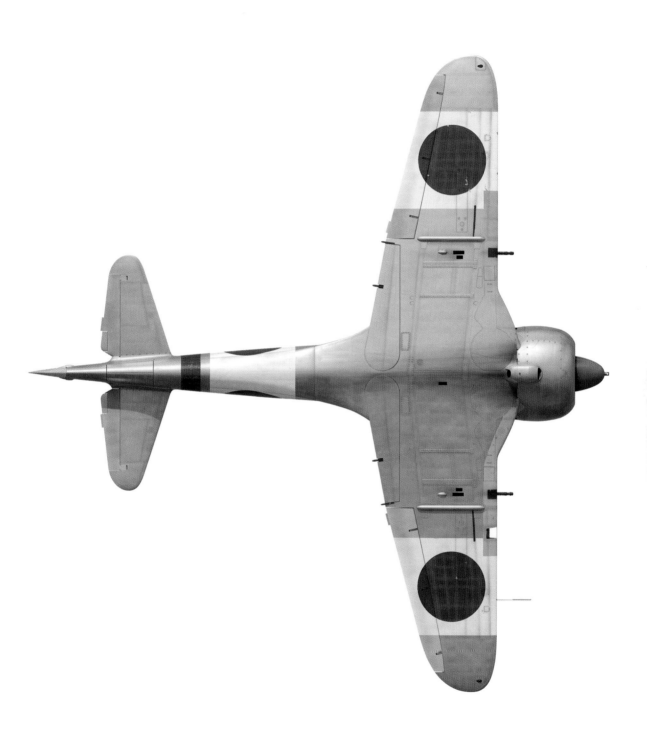

DEFENCE OF THE HOMELAND

When the 47th Chutai returned to Japan following the Doolittle Raid of 18 April 1942, the Ki-44 was still central to the JAAF's concept of air defence. But ironically, during the first raid on the Homeland, it was an aircraft that would succeed the Nakajima interceptor in the JAAF armoury of fighters that was airborne when the B-25s appeared over Tokyo Bay – one of the first examples of the Kawasaki Ki-61 Hien. Japan's first inline engined fighter, the 'Tony', as it was known to the Allies, would play a key role in the coming battle against the B-29s.

However, in 1942 the air defence of Japan had been deliberately neglected in favour of an offensive posture, senior military officers gambling that the capability of the enemy to bomb the Homeland could be pre-empted by territorial gains. In November 1941 the then Army Minister Hideki Tojo had stated his conviction that 'Preparations for Homeland air defence must not interfere with the operations of our armed forces overseas'.

At the time Tojo reported that there were 300 aircraft available for Homeland defence, but this number was misleading. The command structure of the JAAF in Japan was complex, with fighter assets separated under the commands of the IJNAF, General Defence (activated in July 1941, and responsible not just for the defence of Japan but also Korea, Formosa and the Bonin, Ryukyu and Kurile Islands), the Inspectorate General of Army Aviation and the Chief of the Army Aeronautical Department.

Japan itself was divided into four defence districts, with the Northern District covering Hokkaido, the Eastern District covering Honshu from a line north of Shimizu, including Tokyo, the Central District covering Honshu from Shimizu to Yonago, but not the extreme south-western peninsula, and the Western District covering the remainder, including the islands of Kyushu and Shikoku. Of these districts, the Kanto Air Defence Sector occupying the southern half of the Eastern District was considered to be the most vital, as the Kanto Plain area included not just Tokyo, with the Imperial Palace, centres of government and the industrial cities of Yokohama and Kawasaki, but also one of the most important rice producing regions in Japan. It was accorded the highest priority of defence.

Before April 1942, the protection of this vital area was entrusted to a single sentai, the 244th (later to become famous as operators of the Hien), equipped at that time with 50 obsolete Ki-27 'Nates'. The Doolittle Raid demonstrated the inadequacy of this defence, and served as a wake-up call to Imperial General Headquarters. It was ironic that the strike that did so much for Allied morale as the Japanese swept southwards and westwards also contributed to the galvanising of Homeland air defence by exposing the myth that US aircraft would be unable to bomb Japan.

On 30 April 1942 the 17th Air Brigade was formed to protect the Kanto Sector, with two sentais of fighters – the 244th, to transition from the Ki-27 'Nate' to the new Ki-61 'Tony', and the 5th, reduced in size from three to two chutais, and still equipped with the Ki-27. In addition, the returning 47th Chutai was assigned to the brigade, with its Ki-44s duly providing a much-needed punch to the JAAF's air defence capability. This unit would subsequently be increased in size to full sentai status.

The 47th was rated as the most combat effective of the 10th Air Division's fighter assets, being described as the 'best in Division, with many skilled pilots', whereas the 244th Sentai, that has since garnered most of the limelight, was described as only 'Adequate. Second to the 47th in quality'. The 17th Air Brigade was considered part of the 1st Air Army, but was under the direct operational control of the Eastern District Army Command. The 47th's preparation for air defence duties at Narimasu during the early autumn of 1944 included the use of a captured B-17 Flying Fortress for combat training.

By early 1944, in the face of increasing threats to Japan not just from the prospect of B-29 bombing raids but also the wide-ranging carrier task forces of the US Navy, a further strengthening of defences in this vital sector was considered necessary. In March the 17th Air Brigade was reorganised and expanded to become the 10th Air Division, and by July its strength had increased to six air regiments, including the 47th (which had itself been expanded to full sentai strength in October 1943) and the 70th, both equipped with the Ki-44.

The latter sentai had converted to the Shoki in Manchuria in May 1943 as part of the 6th Air Brigade, which was stationed on satellite fields west of Hsingshu. In February 1944, now fully equipped with the Ki-44, the unit was transferred to Kashiwa, in Japan, but in July 1943 it was hastily transferred back to Manchuria in response to the B-29 raids on Anshan (as described in chapter five). The 70th's presence in Japan from February to July 1943 has largely escaped documentation before. When the unit returned to Kashiwa on 6 November 1944, it was not immediately considered combat ready as time was required to bring the 70th's cadre of aircraft up to full serviceability.

Ki-44-II Ko Shokis of the 47th Sentai on Home Defence duties prepare for take-off as groundcrew remove their wheel chocks (*via Henry Sakaida*)

The 23rd Sentai was also established at around this time in an effort to increase the strength of the 10th Air Division. It was formed from within the Ohta Training Air Group, part of the Hitachi Training Air Division, on 11 October 1944. At first the sentai was equipped entirely with Ki-43 'Oscars', but subsequently the 1st Chutai would receive Ki-44s. The 23rd was based at Imba from November, and the unit's top 'B-29

Pilots of the 23rd Sentai's 1st and 2nd Hikotai formally pose with one of the unit's Ki-44s at Imba, Japan, in December 1944 (*Yasuho Izawa*)

killer', TSgt Tomokitsu Yamada, would claim four Superfortresses destroyed by war's end.

The final Shoki component in the air defence preparations was the 246th Sentai, a much-misunderstood unit. From May 1942 it had embodied the main strength of the 18th Air Brigade for organisational purposes, being allocated to the Central District but under the operational control of the Central Army Command. In June 1944, in response to B-29 raids against Kyushu, the 246th was transferred to Ozuki, in the Western District, under the temporary command of the 19th Air Brigade. Part of the unit was also detached to Omura to provide air defence for the Nagasaki area. In early July 1944 the 246th returned to the 18th Air Brigade as part of the latter unit's reorganisation into the 11th Air Division.

Other fighter units serving with the 11th Air Division at this time included the 16th Chutai, equipped with the interceptor version of the twin-engined Ki-46 'Dinah' reconnaissance aircraft, and the 55th and 56th Sentais with the Ki-61 'Tony'.

The 246th Sentai, based at Taisho, was destined for several confusing detachments and reassignments in response to the 'firefighting' forced

A beautiful study of an anonymous Ki-44 in the typical factory finish of the mid-war years. The airframe is unpainted except for the blood-red national insignia and the blue-black anti-glare panel. The propeller was painted a lustrous dark brown and the fabric-covered control surfaces – ailerons, elevators and rudder – were doped in the standard Army grey-green. On this example the leading edge IFF (Identification Friend or Foe) strips, extending to half the length of the wing, appear to be painted red rather than yellow – an exception common to early Home Defence fighters. The optical gunsight in the windscreen has been removed (*Arawasi*)

on the Army Air Headquarters by Allied operations (see chapter five). In November 1944 the 16th Chutai was redesignated the 82nd Sentai and put under the direct command of the 246th. From April 1945 the 246th began to be equipped with the Ki-84.

FIGHTING THE B-29

Combating the B-29 was a most difficult task even for a fighter designed from the outset to perform an air defence role. By the time of the major Superfortress raids on Japan the Ki-44 design was four years old, and had been largely superseded by types designed from scratch to provide general rather than specialist fighter capability, like the Ki-61 'Tony' and Ki-84 'Frank'.

The Ki-44's sparkling rate of climb, whilst still competitive, was only marginally superior to these later fighters, requiring ten minutes less to climb to the B-29's operating altitude of 30,000 ft than the Ki-45 and Ki-61. But this was offset by other disadvantages such as reduced control at that altitude. The Shoki had such high wing-loading that even modest turns at high altitude could result in a dramatic loss of height. The aircraft had an advantage over other fighters because of its excellence as a gun platform, however, and some pilots appreciated the unusual 40 mm armament of the Ki-44-II Otsu.

Overall, the JAAF considered the Ki-44 to be inferior to the Ki-46 and the Ki-61 in general high altitude performance, but superior to the Ki-43 and twin-engined Ki-45.

In the autumn of 1944 the 10th Air Division had held climb-to-height trials as part of the Hitachi Training Air Division's high altitude research. Capt Teisuke Kitagawa's Ki-46 of the 16th Chutai achieved the quickest time – 14 minutes 30 seconds – to 30,000 ft.

The air defence warning system gave at best approximately one hour's notice of the approach of B-29 formations, and most aircraft required this amount of time, or even slightly longer, to take off from a cold start and reach the bombers' altitude. This meant that the fighters were sometimes compelled to attack the B-29s from below or at a steep angle whilst still climbing so as to avoid the defensive fire of the ventral and tail gun turrets.

Any diving attack, if achieved by managing to climb above the Superfortresses, meant a significant loss of altitude, but this was initially offset by the B-29s flying in trail rather than in a staggered formation. This allowed the same fighters to regain altitude after an engagement and attack subsequent waves of bombers.

The head-on attack from slightly above the bomber – thought to be the best means of approach due to the vulnerability of the B-29's cockpit – was also difficult to achieve, requiring careful coordination of interception so that the pilot had sufficient time to turn back into the rapidly closing bomber formation. For all these reasons the downing, or even damaging, of a B-29 was no mean feat.

The idea of ramming attacks was not new to the JAAF when B-29s first appeared over Japan. They had already been used spontaneously or in extremis against Allied bombers in other theatres, and against Superfortresses over Manchuria. An increasing lack of aviation fuel further encouraged the adoption of ramming attacks, as there was little

WO Naoharu Shiromoto was a 21-victory ace who flew briefly with an unknown Ki-44 unit in the defence of Japan during January 1944. This 'specially formed unit' has not been identified. Captured by Soviet forces in Korea, where he was serving in a training unit, WO Shiromoto was imprisoned for his part in the Nomonhan fighting and not released until 1947 (*Yasuho Izawa*)

fuel available for lengthy pilot training in the art of conventional bomber interception by late 1944. It was therefore suggested that, in view of examples from other theatres, pilots should deliberately ram the B-29s.

These desperate tactics would further reduce Japan's dwindling pilot and aircraft assets (although from the outset the pilot was expected, if possible, to parachute to safety or crash-land his aircraft after a ramming attack), but the exchange of a single fighter and relatively inexperienced pilot for a B-29 and its crew was considered a worthwhile price to pay. In addition, the stripping of all armour and weapons from the ramming aircraft improved their performance and increased their chances of positioning to attack the fast, high-flying bombers successfully. On the other hand, the scheme tended to increase the attrition of valuable experienced pilots because the skill required to ram a B-29 successfully was beyond most novice pilots. For this reason several staff officers and unit commanders did not entirely approve of the practice.

AIR-TO-AIR BOMBING

The concept of the air-to-air bombing of compact formations of enemy aircraft in order to break them up and/or disrupt their attacks was not new. The technique originated with IJNAF units in the south-west Pacific, and was held to be a promising means to combat the B-29. Aircraft equipped with bomb racks would fly above enemy formations and drop clusters of small time- or contact-fused bombs in the path of the bombers. The bombs were known as Ta-dan.

The fragmentation weapon was a 40 mm hollow charge streamlined bomb weighing 0.74 lbs that was released in clusters of 30 or 76. Most types of JAAF fighters could be equipped to carry the bombs, but the Ki-46 was found to be the most effective, having the necessary performance to climb above the B-29 formations and shadow them. Both the 47th and 246th Sentais equipped some of their Ki-44s for Ta-dan capability. Although not without some successes, these tactics proved ultimately disappointing against the B-29s, and the method was largely abandoned during 1945.

A Japanese fighter (it appears to be a Ki-61) traces its pursuit curve with a contrail as it attacks a B-29 formation in the full glare of the sun high over Japan. It required nerves of steel to close with these fast, high, mutually supporting formations bristling with remotely controlled 0.50-cal machine guns (*via Henry Sakaida*)

A Ki-44 in Home Defence markings, bearing the emblem of the Utsonomya Army Flying School on its rudder. During the period of Homeland Defence a number of Secondary Provisional Units (Tō Ni Go Butai) were formed within the flying schools with fighter aircraft flown by the instructors to augment air defence. This beautifully clean example has also had its optical gunsight removed (*Summer*)

Tō Ni Go Butai

On 10 May 1944 an emergency reinforcement plan saw the establishment of Tō Ni Go Butai (Secondary Provisional Units) at the various air training and testing establishments. During air alerts these units would use specially designated and painted fighter aircraft manned by instructors and test pilots in order to increase the defensive strength of the division. For the duration of such alerts the designated pilots and aircraft would come under the command of the division. It was estimated that this scheme would provide the 10th Air Division with an additional 90 fighters flown by skilled veteran pilots to combat the B-29 raids.

The Tō units were drawn from the Hitachi advanced fighter training school, which deployed both Ki-44s and Ki-84s, the advanced light bomber training school at Hokoda, which deployed Ki-43s, the 1st Advanced Air Training Unit at Sagami and the Army Air Testing Station at Fussa, the latter providing the contribution of advanced experimental aircraft and weapons systems.

The Hitachi school was formed on 20 June 1944 from the Akeno Fighter School branch at Mito when Akeno was re-formed as an operational unit. Hitachi operated all the main JAAF fighter types, including the Ki-44,

A two-month-old Ki-44-II Ko of the Army Test Centre at Fussa shows off its profile. The marking on the rudder is the Katakana character 'ha' and the three red fuselage stripes may identify this as the third Ko to undertake armament trials at the centre. During the final months of the war several experimental fighter types were flown from Fussa by test pilots on interception sorties (*Picarella Collection*)

forming the 1st and 2nd Kyodo Hikotais (Training Air Units). In December 1944 the 22nd Sentai at Sagami and the 16th Air Brigade at Shimodate (51st and 52nd Sentais) were also designated as Tō units. Although ostensibly equipped with the formidable Ki-84, they were

in the process of reorganisation and working up, with a minimum number of serviceable aircraft.

In practice, the Tō units proved disappointing. Their contribution to air defence was considered to be negligible, while at the same time their creation significantly disrupted training programmes. Ground-to-air communication remained particularly problematic, creating command and control issues for the Tō units. As the B-29 raids intensified, they were relied on less and less, until the scheme was officially abandoned in April 1945.

Ki-44-II Ko serial number 1200, manufactured in April 1943, displays the emblem of the Akeno Training Air Division instructor squad. The last two digits of the aircraft serial number were often painted on the undercarriage fairing and beneath the forward edge of the cowling, but in this case the middle two digits ('20') were applied. The aircraft parked behind the Ki-44s is a Tachikawa Ki-54c 'Hickory' light transport also assigned to the Akeno Training Air Division (*Summer*)

Left
A line up of Ki-44-II Kos, probably from the Akeno Training Air Division. The fighters are wearing the dapple camouflage over natural metal that was typical for the type. At its height, Akeno operated two hikotai of Ki-44 fighters (*Arawasi*)

A splendid in-flight image of an Akeno Army Flying School Ki-44-II Ko. The school's emblem on the rudder is incomplete, as it lacks the character 'Ake' (for Akeno) in the centre. On 20 June 1944 the school was reorganised to perform a combat role for the Air Defence of Japan as the Akeno Kyodo Hiko Shidan (Akeno Training Flying Division) under the command of its former principal Maj Gen Takezou Aoki (*Kikuchi Collection via Hiroshi Umemoto*)

The Tō Ni Go plan should not be confused with the wholesale conversion of training establishments, such as the Akeno Flying Training School, into fighter units.

—— FIRST B-29 RAIDS ON JAPAN ——

The first B-29 raid on Japan was Mission No 1 against the Imperial Iron and Steel Works at Yawata, on Kyushu, on the night of 15/16 June 1944. Some 68 Superfortresses were involved, of which 47 bombed the primary target. Although seven B-29s were lost to various causes during the operation, only one was actually shot down – by a Ki-45 of the 4th Sentai (see *Osprey Aviation Elite Units 5 - B-29 Hunters of the JAAF*).

This first night raid was expected by the 19th Air Division, which had been established that same month at Ozuki for the defence of the strategic industrial areas of northern Kyushu, especially the Yawata Iron and Steel Works. To begin with, the principal aircraft used by the division for night operations were the twin-engined Ki-45 Toryu heavy fighters of the 4th Sentai, of which 25 were operational – ten of these were specially developed nightfighters. There were also at least two 'Dinahs' attached to the Brigade Headquarters that had also been modified as nightfighters.

In addition, the 59th Sentai operated 25 Ki-61s, although these were plagued by technical problems that included fuel vapour locks on take-off and engine stalls during steep dives. Only seven or eight of the aircraft were serviceable. The 59th's pilots were still not fully familiar with the 'Tony' either, and only a handful of them had enough experience with it to fly at night – just four were sortied against the 15/16 June raiders.

The defence sector of the 19th was highly concentrated because it was considered that night defence missions had to be flown in coordination with searchlight batteries, and there were only a limited number of these. As a result, the 19th Air Division HQ formulated very precise operational plans under assigned code names to provide for different combinations of constant standing patrols.

Early warning systems linked to China had given the 19th Air Division HQ advance notice of Mission No 1 at 1530 hrs on the afternoon of 15 June, and the likely course, target and time-on-target of the bombers were very accurately estimated.

At first the results of the air defence that night were interpreted as a resounding success, with seven enemy bombers claimed as being destroyed and four more damaged for no Japanese losses. Later analysis proved that these tallies were too optimistic, and the confirmed enemy losses to air defence were downgraded to only two following intelligence received from China. This more realistic appraisal of the defence capability, and the expectation of daylight raids, prompted the General Defence HQ to reinforce the division with the 16th Air Brigade, consisting of the 51st and 52nd Sentais equipped with the Ki-84 and the 246th Sentai equipped with the Ki-44. The latter unit, based at Ozuki, was allocated the defence of the main strategic area in conjunction with the 4th and 59th Sentais, whilst a detachment from the 246th was to operate from Omura airfield in defence of the Nagasaki area.

The 246th was deployed in a double layer of standing patrols, in coordination with the 4th Sentai, for the night raids on 7/8 July against

A pilot at the Akeno Flying School prepares for a sortie in Ki-44-II Ko '93'. This photograph shows how the retractable steps were used to access the cockpit, but note that the cockpit emergency exit door remains closed. The pilot is wearing a winter flying suit, and his parachute pack has probably already been placed in the seat pan. Sparse green mottle over natural metal was typical for mid-series Shokis, and it displays evidence of touch-up (*Shigeo Hayashi via R C Mikesh*)

A Ki-44-II Ko rolls past the camera for take-off. The pilot is wearing a cotton balaclava under his flying helmet and sunglasses. The Ko's optical (telescopic) gunsight is apparent, the wing gun muzzles are sheathed and a perforated 'blister' for collecting spent cartridge cases is just visible beneath the wing (*Kikuchi Collection via Hiroshi Umemoto*)

Sasebo, Omura, Tobata and Yawata by small groups of aircraft, and again on 10/11 August when 29 bombers hit Nagasaki. However, the 246th was unable to engage the enemy aircraft during these raids, despite the fact that the division had managed to put almost twice the number of aircraft into the air than on the first night raid. There were also no significant B-29 losses in these early missions.

In mid-July 1944 it was realised that the reinforcements to the 19th Air Division required a more comprehensive command structure, so it was subsumed into a new 12th Air Division under the command of Maj Gen Furuya. This reorganisation, completed by 17 July, saw the new division incorporating the 4th and 59th Sentais. Following these changes the 16th Air Brigade and 246th Sentai also remained attached to the 12th Division.

On 20 August the first daylight mission against Yawata was flown by 88 B-29s, of which 71 bombed the primary target. There were a total of 14 losses, including two to a ramming attack. One of the latter bombers was Col Robert Clinkscale's 42-6334 *Gertrude C* of the 468th BG, which was struck by a Ki-45 from the 4th Sentai. After hitting Clinkscale's aircraft, the disintegrating twin-engined fighter collided with Capt Ornell Stauffer's 42-6368 *Calamity Sue*, ripping off its stabiliser and causing the B-29 to fall away out of control. Col Richard Carmichael's 42-24474 of the 462nd BG was hit simultaneously by a fighter from below and an aerial bomb from above. Eight crewmen, including Carmichael, managed to bail out and were captured by the Japanese. They were duly tried as war criminals for bombing civilians but survived the war. Carmichael subsequently led B-29s into combat over Korea six years later.

Immediately after the 20 August raid the 16th Air Brigade and 246th Sentai left the 12th Air Division and returned to their former commands.

Omura was the target for Mission No 13 on 25 October, but there were no losses during the raid by 56 B-29s.

On 1 November the 47th Sentai was in action for the first time over the Homeland when it pursued an F-13 photo-reconnaissance variant of the B-29. This aircraft, from the 3rd Photographic Group, was mapping the Kanto plain area from an altitude of 32,000 ft. The 47th scrambled its available Ki-44s from Narimasu at 1300 hrs and began the long climb to reach the American bomber. In the lead was

Capt Jun Shimizu (1st Chutai commander), but as the Ki-44 formation reached 27,000 ft the aircraft began wallowing in the sky. Some pilots were forced to drop their noses to climb at a shallower angle, while others found themselves stalling out as they climbed. Shimizu and his wingman, 1Lt Shinichi Matsuzaki, managed to get to within 3000 ft of the intruder, and with little hope of hitting it fired short bursts as they struggled to keep their Ki-44s under control.

The B-29 crew reported that some fighters had 'buzzed around' them, but they had not come within range. It was an inauspicious beginning for the Ki-44 in the role of Homeland defender, and although the F-13 was not weighed down with bombs or concerned with formation keeping, the challenge of engaging the high-flying aircraft was only too obvious to the 47th's pilots.

On 6 November the commanding officer of the 10th Air Division, Maj Gen Kihachiro Yoshida, ordered each of the fighter units under his command to form air-to-air ramming flights, called Shinten Seikutai (Heaven Shaking Air Superiority Units), of four aircraft each. These machines were to be specially modified so as to be able to reach altitudes of 30,000 ft under control. This entailed stripping the fighters of armament, fuel tank protection, armour and even gunsights in an effort to lighten them. With these modifications, it was claimed that the Ki-44 could reach 45,000 ft. The Shoki-equipped 23rd, 47th and 70th Sentais responded to this order and began preparing aircraft for ramming attacks. In the 47th Sentai, the Shinten Seikutai consisted of Yoshio Mita, Takayoshi Nagasaki, Isamu Sakamoto and Suguru Suzuki.

On 11 November Omura's aircraft factory on Kyushu was the target for 94 B-29s, but bad weather and cloud resulted in a diversion to Nanking and only 30 aircraft bombed the primary target. They were scattered, could not see the target and were hampered by turbulence. Although there was little defence offered by the Japanese, five B-29s were reported lost or missing.

Mission No 17 took the B-29s back to Omura on 21 November, with 63 bombers encountering a more aggressive air defence. One B-29 was shot down, another was listed as missing in action and several more were damaged, including a Superfortress that was hit by an air-to-air rocket in the Central Fire Control compartment. The gunnery system of the bomber was destroyed, with one gunner killed instantly and

A trio of Akeno Ki-44-II Ko aircraft taxi out from the flightline at the start of a sortie. The 'butterfly' combat flaps beneath the wings have been dropped 15 degrees for take-off. For landing they were also set at 15 degrees, and for deployment in combat turns during flight, nine degrees. Also visible beneath the starboard wing of the nearest aircraft is an aerial gun camera, which was used mainly during training sorties (*Kikuchi Collection via Hiroshi Umemoto*)

Capt Jun Shimizu, 1st Chutai leader of the 47th Sentai, led the interception mission on 1 November 1944 against the first F-13 (B-29) photo-reconnaissance aircraft to sortie over Tokyo. The Superfortress was cruising at 32,000 ft, and the JAAF pilots found that they could barely control their Ki-44s at that altitude (*via Henry Sakaida*)

An early morning start up as groundcrew prepare 1st Chutai aircraft of the 70th Sentai for the day's flying. The aircraft in the foreground is serial number 1377, which was part of the first batch of Ki-44-II Heis manufactured in August 1943 (*Kikuchi Collection via Hiroshi Umemoto*)

Ki-44s of the 47th Sentai are prepared for flight in Japan. This sentai was the longest serving Shoki unit, and in Home Defence it was rated the 'best in Division, with many skilled pilots'. The sentai emblem – a stylised design of the numbers '4' and '7' – was painted in different colours to distinguish each chutai (*Yasuho Izawa*)

another thrown from the aircraft. The tail gunner was also seriously wounded and the rudder so badly damaged that the controls had to be tied down to keep the bomber level. The B-29 eventually crash-landed in China.

Last Resort, skippered by Maj Donald Roberts, ran a gauntlet of coordinated fighter attacks by three aircraft which resulted in three of its four engines being shot out. The Superfortress was hounded by more fighters as it lost height and fell away from the main formation. In a desperate fight, the B-29's gunners claimed three attacking fighters shot down and two probables before the flight engineer was able to get one of the engines started again. With the Japanese fighters giving up the attack, the aircraft was stripped of weight and managed to reach a tiny landing field at Laohokao, in China. There, the crew patched the B-29 up using salvaged parts from a Superfortress that had force-landed earlier, and the following day the aircraft returned safely to base.

The first daylight attack on Tokyo was mounted on 24 November by B-29s of XXI Bomber Command, which was operating from newly completed bases in the Marianas. A total of 175 Superfortresses bombed docks and urban area, as well as the Musashino Nakajima aircraft factory and targets of opportunity. The 47th Sentai's Shinten Seikutai went into action above Tokyo, with Cpl Yoshio Mita's Ki-44 ramming the tail section of 1Lt Sam Wagner's 42-24622 *Lucky Irish* of the 497th BG, shearing off the starboard stabiliser.

Just moments prior to Mita's attack another Ki-44 flown by the 47th Sentai commander, Maj Noboru Okuda, had raked the B-29 with 40 mm cannon fire in a head-on pass from above the bomber. Other B-29 crews in the formation reported that there was no defensive gunfire as Mita flew into the bomber's tail, wobbling in the B-29's turbulence as he closed on his target. Both aircraft spun away, and there were no parachutes seen. Gunners in another B-29 had begun firing at Mita at a distance of 800 yards as he approached, and they watched in horror as the Ki-44 hit the bomber. Tail gunner Cpl Fred Lodovici in 42-24616 *Haley's Comet* saw the ramming;

'He came in to about 150 or 200 yards just about even with the tail of Ship No 26, and at that time our right gunner opened fire also. He appeared to hover for a while in mid-air and then rolled over the tail, his right wing hitting the vertical stabiliser, and then he rose up into the air and slid onto the left elevator. Then they both went down.'

Despite this success, other Ki-44s from the unit struggled to make an impression on the Superfortresses. Indeed, in the eyes of Maj Todd, piloting 42-24544 *Long Distance* of the 498th BG, the fighter attacks seemed 'feeble and fluttering', with several aircraft attempting to reach his B-29 from behind and below but only one managing to climb up to the bomber's altitude. Once there, it stayed out of range of the tail turret. MSgt Isamu Sakamoto of the 47th's ramming flight attempted to engage a B-29, but he was shot down before he could ram it. His was one of five fighters lost in the attack, and a second ramming by a 17th Chutai 'Dinah' was also reported. After the poor performance of the defending fighters, Maj Gen Yoshida ordered the units to double the number of aircraft prepared for air-to-air ramming to eight per sentai.

On 1 December a single chutai from the 23rd Sentai was sent to Iwo Jima to provide a fighter escort for convoys attempting to resupply Japanese troops defending the beleaguered island. By 26 December every single Ki-44 was either damaged or unserviceable, so the surviving pilots returned to Japan aboard an IJNAF transport aircraft.

On 3 December the 73rd BW targeted the Nakajima aircraft plant at Musashino with 86 B-29s, 60 of which bombed the primary target. Six Superfortresses were lost and 13 damaged during the raid. One of the aircraft downed was 42-24656 *Rosalia Rocket*, flown by Maj Robert Goldsworthy. Attacked over the target just before bomb release by 15 fighters, it was carrying not just the 500th BG commander, Col Richard King, but also Col Bryon Brugge of 73rd BW Headquarters. As it went down the bomber was rammed by the Ki-45 of Sgt Masami Sawamoto of the 53rd Sentai.

1Lt Donald Dufford's 42-24544 *Long Distance* was rammed unintentionally by a Ki-61 of the 244th Sentai whose pilot was making a head-on attack. Cpl Misao Itagaki was thrown clear in the collision and parachuted safely to the ground. His smashed fighter cartwheeled over the B-29's wing and reportedly hit another 'Tony', with both aircraft 'going down in flames'. In reality, *Long Distance* managed to make it safely back to base.

1Lt Charles E Fetter's B-29 42-24735 was rammed over the target by Cpl Matsumi Nakano of the 244th after he had made two unsuccessful attacks on other aircraft, the Japanese pilot surviving the collision to crash-land. The stricken bomber lost height and was attacked by other fighters, including IJNAF aircraft, before finally being abandoned by its crew over the sea. The 10th Air Division claimed four B-29s destroyed by ramming for the loss of six aircraft and one pilot.

The six pilots of the 23rd Sentai's Iwo Jima detachment. Originally, 12 aircraft of the unit's 3rd Hikotai had been sent to the island, but six were lost en route. WO Tomoo Yamada, second from right in the rear row, was the acting leader of the detachment. To his right is TSgt Tomokitsu Yamada, the unit's leading B-29 killer, credited with three bombers destroyed – he claimed four, however (*Yasuho Izawa*)

Capt Tadayoshi Watabe (2nd Chutai leader) briefs 70th Sentai Ki-44 pilots before an air defence patrol. The blackboard displays the flight formation, with aircraft flown by Capt Watabe, Cpl Saburo Hirahara, Sgt Koji Namba and MSgts Katsuzo Ichida and Ken-ichi Hiratsuka (*Kikuchi Collection via Hiroshi Umemoto*)

Maj Yoshio Hirose flew Ki-44s in the 1st Hikotai of the Hitachi Training Air Division during the defence of Japan. He had claimed a total of nine victories by the time he was killed in a ramming attack on a B-29 on 22 December 1944 (*Yasuho Izawa*)

As the bombers left the target area the 498th BG was attacked by Ki-44s of the 70th Sentai over the Izu peninsula. MSgt Ken-ichi Hiratsuka, who had already engaged B-29s over Manchuria, attacked a Superfortress. He knew that the bombers would probably descend after they had attacked their target, so he waited until the formation was below him before making a head-on diving run against a B-29 from above. Hiratsuka succeeded in setting the aircraft's No 3 engine alight, but the bomber stayed aloft.

South-east of Tokyo, eight Ki-44s of the 47th Sentai also attacked the B-29s and damaged two of them, pilots reporting seeing white smoke being trailed by these machines. 1st Chutai leader Capt Sunao Shimizu, flying alone, attacked a B-29 formation at 27,000 ft, and despite his Ki-44 being hit by defensive fire, he claimed two as damaged – one of these flew off trailing a plume of black smoke. On this occasion the claims seemed reasonable, for B-29 42-24681 of the 498th BG ditched in the sea with combat damage and another bomber from the group, 42-63383, crash-landed. A fourth Superfortress, 42-63432 *Lucky Irish* also from the 498th BG, ditched on its way home after running out of fuel.

The bombing results from this mission had been so poor that the 73rd BW went back to Musashino on 27 December with 72 B-29s. Only 39 managed to bomb the primary target, and three Superfortresses were lost. The 70th Sentai's Ki-44s were up against this raid, but the results they achieved remain unknown.

On 9 January the bombers attacked Musashino for a fifth time, sending out 72 B-29s, but only 18 were able to attack the primary target – poor weather forced the Superfortresses to bomb by radar. Secondary targets were attacked by 34 B-29s.

The 47th Sentai scrambled from Narimasu to intercept the bombers. Sgt Masami Yuki, intent on destroying a B-29, ripped out an engine from one of the Superfortresses when he rammed it. Killed in the process, Yuki's body was found in a field near Tokyo, close to the B-29's engine. The stricken bomber fell out of formation and was set upon by more Shokis from the 47th, led by 2nd Chutai leader Capt Yasuro Mazaki. WO Takashi Awamura attacked Yuki's victim, and seeing there was no defensive fire from the bomber's gun turrets, he drove his propeller into its wing flaps. The B-29 was seen to dive towards the sea off Choshi Point. Awamura bailed out of his Ki-44 but was never found. Sgt Masumi Sachi of the 47th was also reported killed after ramming a B-29.

Six Superfortresses were lost, at least two of which had been rammed – 42-24665 *Satan's Sister* of the 499th BG (reported as *Miss Behavin* in some accounts) and 42-24772 of the 497th BG. Three B-29s failed to return after they were forced to ditch – 42-24598 *Waddy's Wagon* of the 497th BG, 42-24657 *Mus'n Touch* of the 500th BG and 42-24658

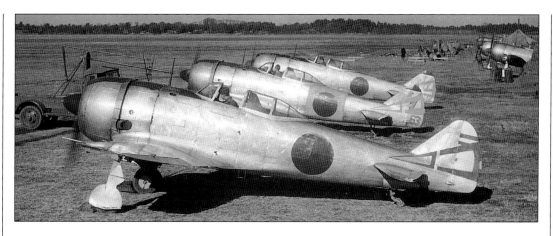

A trio of 70th Sentai Ki-44s are run up by mechanics using a Toyota KC truck. The latter had a power take-off driving a shaft above the cab that was connected to the lug on the spinner in order to start the engine. These vehicles were used to start many different JAAF aircraft types, and they were a common sight on airfields. Aircraft '12' and '63' show evidence of former ownership by the 47th Sentai (*Shigeo Hayashi via R C Mikesh*)

Sgt Masami Yuki of the 47th Sentai rams a B-29 over Narimasu, Japan, on 9 January 1945. Yuki was killed in this attack, while the stricken Superfortress fell out of formation under continuous attack by other 47th Sentai 'Tojos' led by Capt Yasuro Mazaki. WO Takashi Awamura finally rammed the bomber to bring it down into the sea (*Yasuho Izawa*)

Wugged Wascal of the 499th BG. The sixth B-29 lost might have been 42-24744 of the 500th BG.

The 73rd BW targeted the Musashino factory for a sixth time on 27 January with at least 116 B-29s, of which 106 bombed the primary or secondary targets (the docks and urban area of Tokyo). Seven squadrons participated in the mission, and they were to attack either the Nakajima factory at Musashino or the Mitsubishi factory at Nagoya depending on the weather over the target. Two weather-monitoring B-29s were sent out to transmit target information en route. None of the aircraft ultimately bombed the primary target, although 62 of them ran the gauntlet of an estimated 900 fighter attacks, more than half of which targeted the 497th BG.

The 47th Sentai was up, and its Ki-44s joined Ki-61s from the 244th Sentai in attacks on the bomber formations. The Shokis made repeated gunnery runs on Col Robert 'Pappy' Haynes' 42-24623 *Thumper* of the 870th BS. Nevertheless, the badly damaged B-29 made it home – the only one of four aircraft from the squadron to do so. Bombardier Raleigh Phelps reckoned that the B-29 had been subjected to more than 100 attacks, 57 of them from the front quarter. Some Ki-44s and Ki-61s came only to within 400 yards of the bomber and then turned or dived away, but others were so close that they cleared it by just a few feet.

Sgt Maj Kiyoshi Suzuki of the 47th flew head-on into Capt Raymond Dauth's 42-24619 *Shady Lady* of the 497th BG on the way to the target. The B-29 lurched from the impact and Dauth tried to regain control, but the bomber fell away on fire and was never seen again. Suzuki's Ki-44 plunged into a river at Oume, killing the pilot.

After 1Lt Edward G 'Snuffy' Smith's 42-24769 *Rover Boy Express* was fatally hit by 37 mm cannon fire from a Ki-45 'Nick', it was continuously attacked by Ki-44s

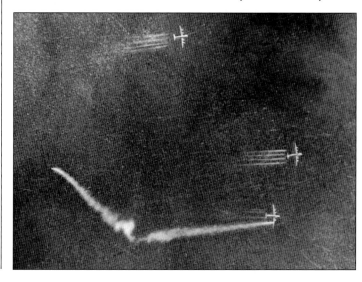

as it fell away. The B-29 crashed into Ikisu village near the IJNAF airfield at Konoiki, with five of the crew being killed, along with seven villagers. Seven crewmen managed to bail out, including the pilot.

After being shot down by a B-29 turret gunner two months earlier, 23-year-old MSgt Isamu Sakamoto of the 47th Sentai's Shinten Seikutai was determined to down a bomber this time. At 30,000 ft he approached the leading B-29 in the second box of a formation of 70 aircraft. He missed his quarry during his first run at the bombers, and as he turned in for a second attempt his Ki-44 was hit and the main fuel tank burst into flames. Ignoring the blaze, Sakamoto continued his run and rammed a B-29 that was subsequently reported to have crashed near Inhan-numa. He was thrown clear in the collision, and although injured, made a safe parachute descent. Sakamoto survived but never flew again. Gen Keisuke Fujie, the commanding general of the Eastern District, awarded Sakamoto the Bukosho 2nd Class for this ramming attack.

In total, the Japanese fighters claimed 22 B-29s downed, but in reality only nine had been lost. Ten ramming attacks were made, resulting in the deaths of five pilots, with four more bailing out successfully and one force-landing his damaged aircraft. In addition to Sgt Maj Suzuki of the 47th, Sgt Hajime Yoshida of the 70th was also killed flying a Ki-44, although the circumstances leading to his death are unknown.

On 27 January 12 more Ki-44s from the 23rd Sentai were again sent to Iwo Jima for convoy escort duties, and by 8 February most of them had been lost and the detachment ordered to return to its main force.

Two days later, sometime after 1300 hrs, WO Makoto Ogawa of the Kashiwa-based 3rd Chutai of the 70th Sentai was patrolling over Mt Fuji at 30,000 ft in his Ki-44 when his formation was alerted to another bomber raid approaching Tokyo from Kashima Nada. Ogawa was a veteran of the Manchurian fighting, and he had tangled with the B-29s before. Graduating as a pilot in 1938, the 27-year-old warrant officer had served as a flying instructor at Kumagaya prior to joining the 70th Sentai at the

RIGHT:
By early 1944 the JAAF's standard flight (shotai) formation had become four aircraft flying in two pairs, rather than the obsolete 'vic' of three. Highly experienced Akeno instructors like Maj Kan Tashiro – the 'Master of the Heavy Fighter' – were instrumental in teaching both the new formations and the hit-and-run tactics that exploited the performance of the Ki-44. Maj Tashiro believed that the success of the new 'Rotte' tactics (from the Luftwaffe term for a pair) was dependent on the speed and armament of the Ki-44 (*Kikuchi Collection via Hiroshi Umemoto*)

A 70th Sentai 3rd Chutai Ki-44-II Hei in flight over the Kanto Plain. This aircraft appears to have had its wing armament removed. The 70th was equipped with the Shoki until war's end (*Kikuchi Collection via Hiroshi Umemoto*)

end of 1941. Participating in the defence of the Homeland from November 1944 until war's end, Ogawa would become one of the 70th Sentai's most successful pilots, eventually claiming seven B-29s and two P-51 Mustangs shot down.

Taking advantage of the jetstream wind over Japan, Ogawa and his comrades headed towards the bombers' target, Ota, where they managed to catch up with the rear formation of a combined force of 98 B-29s from the 73rd and 313th BWs. The Superfortress crews had been tasked with flattening Ota's Nakajima aircraft factory, where the formidable Ki-84 'Frank' fighter was being built.

Ogawa dived straight through the B-29 formation and then zoomed up to attack the bombers from below, firing a short burst at an aircraft with its bomb-bay doors already open. Whether Ogawa's fire detonated the B-29's bombs, or it was hit by flak at the same time or from an overhead attack by 2Lt Toshizo Kurai of the 1st Training Unit from Sagami (who also claimed his victim had collided with another Superfortress after being hit), or whether this was an entirely separate incident may never be known. There was a colossal explosion and B-29 42-24784 *Slick's Chicks*, flown by Capt Carmel Slaughter Jr of the

Heikichi Yoshizawa of the 47th Sentai (seen here in front of a Ki-84 Hayate) had already claimed three B-29s shot down when he rammed a fourth over Ota on 10 February 1945, killing himself in the process (Yasuho Izawa)

505th BG, fell away and collided with 1Lt Owen Barnhart Jr's 42-24815 *Deaner Boy*. Both aircraft were lost, crashing into Takashima village in Gunma prefecture. Ogawa and Kurai (the latter pilot now a B-29 ace with claims for five of the bombers brought down) were separately credited.

42-24867 *Sassy Lassy* of the 505th BG was separated from its formation by a series of fighter attacks. One fighter coming in from '11 o'clock' as though intending to ram the B-29 caused the pilot to pull out of formation to avoid a collision, and Japanese pilots were able to exploit the gap to concentrate on the lone bomber. The last time it was seen, *Sassy Lassy* was under attack by at least ten fighters.

Ki-44s from the 47th Sentai also intercepted the Ota-bound Superfortresses, the unit's 1Lt Heikichi Yoshizawa flying straight at a formation inverted, before rolling upright and flashing across the top of the B-29s. Barely 30 ft above the bombers, he slammed his Shoki into one of them. Yoshizawa's wingman, 2Lt Ryozo Ban, followed him into the formation, but his Ki-44 was hit by defensive fire. With a damaged engine, Ban had to break away and make an emergency landing at Shimodate.

Prior to take-off, Yoshizawa, convinced that he would destroy one of the big American bombers, had pinned a small doll to his flying suit as a good luck charm, and he had told Ban 'Follow me today!' Ban had replied that he would follow Yoshizawa to heaven or hell.

No fewer than 12 B-29s were reported lost following the Ota mission, five of them ditching on their return journey. Two of the latter aircraft had run out of fuel.

HELLCATS VERSUS SHOKIS

On 15 February 117 B-29s headed for the Mitsubishi factory at Nagoya 24 hours before carrier strike forces were scheduled to hit the Tokyo area. The mission was disrupted by a weather front and only 33 bombers hit the primary target, with one reported lost.

The following day the aircraft of TF 38 conducted a series of sweeps over Japanese airfields around Tokyo. Both IJNAF and JAAF fighters were up in force, and hectic dogfights erupted resulting in scores of claims and counter claims. Amongst the Japanese pilots lost to Hellcats from VF-80 over Imba were Maj Juro Fujita, the CO of the 23rd Sentai, who was flying a Ki-43 'Oscar', WO Shigeo Nakayama, Sgt Maj Yoshiji Okazaki and two others from the same unit. In return, the Commander Air Group (CAG) from USS *Lexington* (CV-16), Cdr Phil Torrey Jr, was last seen climbing and then diving out of control after making a head-on pass at a 'Tojo' in his Hellcat. His wingman from VF-9 stalled out before he could come to the aid of his CAG, and after recovering his F6F he did not see his leader again. Torrey failed to return.

As the 23rd Sentai bounced the Hellcats of VF-9 from their 'six o'clock high' position, they were spotted by ace Lt Gene Valencia in his rear-view mirror. The US Navy pilots flung themselves into a hard climbing turn, and Torrey, having outdistanced the others, tackled the 'Tojos' head on. Coming up hard, but still out of range, Valencia salvoed four of his underwing rockets at one of the oncoming Ki-44s, but all of them fell away short. However, fellow ace Lt Harris Mitchell fired accurately into the engine of a 'Tojo' that was heading straight for him, causing it to burst into flames. As he pulled up over the burning fighter the Japanese pilot bailed out. Following this clash two of VF-9's Hellcats failed to return to CV-16.

On 17 February another series of sweeps and strikes were launched by TF 38, this time claiming the life of Capt Kensui Kono, the 70th's 3rd Chutai leader and an ace with nine B-29s to his credit. Over Atsugi, TSgt Sadao Miyazawa of the 70th Sentai evened up the score by downing an F6F. His Ki-44 was subsequently marked with an eagle, its wings outstretched, on the fuselage to denote this victory. That evening MSgt Ken-ichi Hiratsuka of the 70th Sentai's 3rd Chutai also claimed an Hellcat – one of four shot down over Atsugi.

As the B-29 raids on Japan increased in their intensity in early 1945, and the first carrier strikes were made against the Homeland, it was decided to concentrate all the air defences under a single command organisation. Consequently, the Air General Army (AGA) was established on 15 April under the command of Gen Masajazu Kawabe. The 1st Air Army that had been responsible for training and personnel replacement was made an operational command and assigned the 10th Air Division. This new structure incorporated the 70th Sentai, but lost the 47th Sentai, which was transferred to the newly formed 30th Fighter Group, together with the 244th Sentai and 17th Chutai.

The 30th had been formed to defend the Kanto sector in place of the 6th Air Army, which now came under the command of the Combined Fleet for the defence of the Ryukyu Islands. It moved its operations base to Kyushu.

Capt Kensui Kono, the 70th Sentai's 3rd Chutai leader, prepares for flight. The oxygen mask was usually worn from take-off. Capt Kono was killed in action engaging US Navy Hellcats on 17 February 1945 (*Kikuchi Collection via Hiroshi Umemoto*)

The USAAF bomber commands were also making plans. After two test incendiary missions that had proven inconclusive, a maximum-effort incendiary attack on Tokyo was scheduled for 25 February. Of the 230 B-29s sent to attack the Japanese capital, 172 of them dropped their bombs and burned out a full square mile of urban Tokyo.

Despite the apparent success of this mission, a further conventional raid on Musashino was planned – the eighth to be mounted against the same target. When the raid went in on 4 March heavy cloud cover diverted the B-29s to bomb secondary targets, and the fate of

high altitude precision bombing over Japan was sealed. During early March, with some misgivings, B-29 crews began flying exploratory night missions over Japanese cities, combining small scale bombing raids with radar photo-mapping in preparation for large-scale future missions.

On 9 March 334 B-29s went to Tokyo and 282 of them bombed from 7000 ft, burning out an area of 15.8 square miles and killing an estimated 78,660 people, mostly civilians. The results were shocking, but paved the way for future operations. The irony was that the desperate defence of the Japanese fighters against the high-altitude, precision raids had contributed, in part, to the change of tactics. On that dreadful night of inflagration no B-29s were reported lost to the few nightfighters struggling to make a difference, although flak had downed 14 and damaged 40 more. Or had it?

Amongst those few Japanese fighters weaving through the searchlight beams had been WO Makoto Ogawa of the 70th Sentai, flying a Ki-44-II Otsu armed with 40 mm wing cannon. In the darkness and glare he made repeated runs on B-29s, claiming one shot down and several more damaged. Ogawa's fellow 70th Sentai B-29 hunter Yoshio Yoshida was also credited with the destruction of a bomber that night too. He had destroyed a Superfortress over Manchuria six months earlier, and he would go on to down four more by the end of May. He too would be awarded the Bukosho for his service in defending the Homeland.

Ogawa was a 28-year-old veteran with long flying but little combat

*A JAAF pilot strikes a pose in front of his Shoki. He is wearing winter flying gear, consisting of a padded flight suit and fur-lined helmet. The Shoki displays a sparse mottle camouflage over the natural metal, which was typical for fighter types (*Shigeo Hayashi via R C Mikesh*)*

Although not usually associated with nocturnal sorties, both the 70th and 246th Sentais used the Shoki successfully as a nightfighter. Here, a Ki-44-II Hei of the 70th prepares for another night mission (*Kikuchi Collection via Hiroshi Umemoto*)

The Bukosho (full title Bukochoso) was a Japanese Army decoration for gallantry instituted by Imperial edict on 7 December 1944. Only awarded for the most exemplary acts of courage in combat, the Bukosho could be presented by a commander in the field without the lengthy process of citation submission and approval required for other decorations. The metal badge was usually worn on the lower left breast of the uniform. The award had two classes, the Ko (or first) class in silver and the Otsu (or second) class in bronze (*via Henry Sakaida*)

Another B-29 ace and Bukosho winner of the 70th Sentai was WO Makoto Ogawa, seen here in front of his victory-marked Ki-44. His final score of seven Superfortresses destroyed also included night victories. Ogawa's preferred, but risky, method of attack was from head-on and beneath the bombers. Towards the end of the war he added two P-51 Mustangs to his score (*via Henry Sakaida*)

experience who had joined the 70th in Manchuria in 1941 after a successful three-year stint as a flying instructor. He had originally been destined for a career as a bomber pilot, but his determination and aggressive flying singled him out as fighter pilot material. Whilst serving with the 70th Sentai, Ogawa was one of two aces who perfected nocturnal interceptions with the Ki-44. He preferred to approach his targets from the frontal quarter and below, then rake the belly of the bomber at close range with 40 mm cannon fire – an exceptionally risky tactic. On 9 July 1945 Ogawa was also awarded the Bukosho for his seven B-29 kills and two P-51 Mustang victories, the latter machines having been downed in daylight engagements following the appearance of long-range USAAF fighters over Japan.

Two days after the devastating Tokyo raid on 9 March, the B-29s targeted Nagoya with incendiaries. Only one bomber was lost, the Superfortress ditching due to mechanical failure shortly after take-off. Osaka was hit on the night of 13/14 March, and MSgt Kenji Fujimoto of the 246th Sentai claimed to have deliberately collided with one of the raiders over the city, bringing it down and then parachuting to safety. His victim might well have been Lt Stanley Black's 42-24913 *Thunderin' Loretta* of the 9th BG, whose crew reported being hit by two blasts from the ground shortly after turning away from the target. The B-29 fell out of control – at one point inverted – for several minutes, but eventually the crew regained control and the badly damaged bomber was nursed back to base. Two other Superfortresses were reported lost on this mission.

On the night of 14/15 March 330 B-29s headed for Kobe, and the Shokis of the 246th Sentai again took off from Taisho in the dark to challenge them. Both Kenji Fujimoto and Sgt Yukio Ikuta were credited with making successful ramming attacks, and three B-29s were recorded as lost, two attributed to ramming. Maj Bob Fitzgerald's 42-24849 of the 500th BG was rammed by Capt Junichi Ogata of the 56th Sentai in a Ki-61, the JAAF pilot being killed in the attack. B-29 42-24849 *Mission to Albuquerque* of the 500th BG was also reported as lost to ramming.

For these two ramming attacks, and another B-29 claimed shot down, Kenji Fujimoto was also awarded the Bukosho.

The night of 19/20 March marked the last mission of the fire blitz, as 290 B-29s burned out three square miles of Nagoya. In five maximum effort raids over ten days the bombers had burned 32 square miles of four of Japan's biggest cities. For the next few weeks much of the B-29 effort would be diverted to mining Japan's harbours and bombing targets in Kyushu to support the landings on Okinawa, whilst main force streams continued to attack cities and factories.

On 24/25 March a test mission for precision bombing at night was flown against the Mitsubishi factory at Nagoya. Imitating the RAF's pathfinder techniques, ten B-29s illuminated the target with flares for ten more to ignite marker fires for the 500+ main force to bomb on. The test was not a success, as a combination of cloud and smoke obscured the target area. Five B-29s were also lost to flak or fighters.

MSgt Kenji Fujimoto, a Bukosho winner of the 246th Sentai, shot down a B-29 and rammed another on the night of 13/14 March 1945, surviving this engagement to ram another Superfortress three nights later. He was shot down and killed by P-51 Mustangs on 14 August 1945 whilst flying a Ki-84 Hayate (*via Henry Sakaida*)

Ki-44s of the 246th Sentai in Japan. The first three aircraft in the front row have the painted cowl flaps that were a distinction applied to some Shokis serving with this unit, although the reason why this marking was applied remains obscure. Note also the narrow fuselage band and dark-painted rudder on aircraft '15'. The significance of the various coloured trims applied to the 246th's 'Tojos' is not fully understood (*Yasuho Izawa*)

The former Kawasemi Butai and 64th Sentai ace Maj Yasuhiko Kuroe was airborne that night in a Kawasaki Ki-102, which was an experimental variant of a limited production twin-engined fighter armed with a 57 mm cannon. Kuroe claimed two B-29s destroyed, his victims possibly being 42-63493 *Star Duster* of the 499th BG and 44-69748 *Lil Iodine II* of the 9th BG.

The pathfinder test mission was followed by two smaller repeats by the 314th BW against the Mitsubishi factory and the 73rd BW against the Musashino Nakajima plant, but again the results were disappointing. On 7 April these two targets were hit again in daylight raids in near perfect conditions. The B-29s went in at lower altitudes to bomb and the 73rd BW was accompanied by the first P-51 fighter escorts to appear over Japan, flying long-range missions from Iwo Jima.

Japanese fighter units had already been advised to avoid combat with their USAAF counterparts in order to concentrate on the interception of bombers, and to conserve strength for the expected final defence of the Homeland against invasion. This did not prevent several engagements between Mustangs and 'Tojos', with the 23rd, 70th and 246th Sentais all losing aircraft to the American fighters, but no pilots were reported killed. Despite the protective dogfights, the bombing force lost at least ten Superfortresses, of which three were brought down over Japan by ramming and another by an aerial bomb.

The Tokyo Arsenal was the target for 348 Superfortresses on the night of 13/14 April, with 327 of them bombing. Yoshio Yoshida of the 70th Sentai, up in a Ki-44-II Otsu armed with 40 mm cannon, claimed one of the B-29s shot down out of seven lost. Two nights later Yoshida claimed a second Superfortress victory when 194 aircraft bombed the urban area of Kawasaki. The mission was costly, with 12 B-29s being lost – ten of them to fighters or flak. 42-24664 *Ramblin' Roscoe* of the 500th BG was also badly damaged by fighters, having two of its engines knocked out and the main undercarriage damaged. The bomber made it back to Iwo Jima but crashed on landing.

On the night of 23/24 May TSgt Tomokitsu Yamada, who had been a member of the 23rd's Shinten Seikutai air-to-air ramming flight, went up against a 500+ B-29 mission against Tokyo and claimed three victories. Yoshio Yoshida of the 70th Sentai was credited with two more of the bombers for his fourth and fifth B-29 victories. TSgt Kiyoshi

Capt Yoshio Yoshida was one of the leading B-29 aces of the 70th Sentai, a Home Defence unit. All his confirmed B-29 victories were scored at night, and he is seen here standing in front of a Ki-44 elaborately marked with each of his victories. In the JAAF, successful night interception sorties were considered the mark of an exceptionally skilled fighter pilot (*via Henry Sakaida*)

One of Capt Yoshida's aircraft, in this case a Ki-44-II Hei. The Sentai tail emblem is usually depicted in yellow, but recent research in Japan has confirmed that it was in fact red. Although Capt Yoshida is usually listed as the 3rd Chutai leader, he actually led the 1st Chutai, and the red flash on the leading edge of the fin signifies his leadership status. The chutai colours for this unit were 1st red, 2nd blue and 3rd yellow (*via Henry Sakaida*)

Otaki, also from the 70th, claimed a Superfortress too. Maj Kuroe was in the air again that night, this time in a Ki-84-I Ko Hayate. He claimed another two B-29s downed. A total of 11 bombers were lost to enemy action, of which three were shot down, two crashed over the target to unknown causes and two were listed as missing in action.

The 24-year-old Capt Yoshio Yoshida had graduated from the Army Air Academy in 1939, and after completing fighter training at Akeno he had spent his entire service career with the 70th Sentai, distinguishing himself over Manchuria against the first B-29 raids. After the death of Capt Kohno on 17 February, Capt Yoshida was appointed as 3rd Chutai leader to replace him. By war's end he was preparing to fly the rocket-powered Shusui interceptor (based on the Messerschmitt Me 163).

The following night (24/25 May) Yoshida claimed his sixth B-29. Tokyo was again the target for 498 Superfortresses, of which 464 bombed and no fewer than 26 were reported lost. At least three were brought down by flak, one exploded in the air over Tokyo, five were shot down, seven crashed in Japan to unknown causes, one ditched on its way home with combat damage and two were listed as missing. More than 100 B-29s had also been damaged over a target that was obscured by cloud and smoke. In addition to the nightfighters and flak, crews reported being attacked by parachute bombs and suicide rocket aircraft – the latter were possibly air-to-air rockets fired by nightfighters. WO Tomoo Yamada of the 23rd Sentai, hunting over the target area in a Ki-44, was shot down and killed.

On 5 June Kobe was the target for 524 B-29s, of which 494 attacked the primary target or targets of opportunity. The bombing force went in during daylight and at 18,000 ft, losing 11 B-29s to fighters and flak. To the bomber crews the fighter attacks were as vicious and relentless as ever, combining gunnery runs and ramming attacks. B-29 pilot Ivan Potts described an attack by a 40 mm armed Ki-44-II Otsu (identified erroneously as an IJNAF 'George');

'The thing I remember most of all was this ["Tojo"] fighter. As we were coming in on the target we were flying lead aeroplane in the right hand flight of the lead flight, and we could see this ["Tojo"] fighter circling around down below us. All at once he decided to make his move. He pulled up and he circled around in front of us, and you could almost tell that he had picked us out. As he came in level against us he rolled that baby over, with its big round group of cylinders that reminded me of an old Gee Bee sportster like Col Roscoe Turner used to fly back in the "thirties".

'This was a beautiful day – it was as clear as could be. He was out several hundred yards, and he headed right in our direction, closing on us at a tremendous rate of speed. He rolled that ["Tojo"] onto its back and fired two 40 mm cannons at us and headed straight down. All the time our new bombardier was pointing and saying "Look at him come", and, as I remember I said, "Look at him! Hell – shoot, shoot!" but nothing ever happened. I don't think we got a shot at him from the nose.

'One of the cannon shells hit our left outboard engine. It was a monstrous shell and that engine went out immediately – we were able to feather it. The other shell hit us absolutely in the middle of the bomb-bay. This was only about 15 or 20 seconds after the bombs had gone. Later on our groundcrew told us that they counted 148 holes in the bomb-bay of the aeroplane. And of course, we really figured we were in trouble at that time. We didn't know whether we were going down, whether we were going to be able to keep that baby up there, or just what in the world was going to happen.'

Potts and his crew managed to get back to Iwo Jima, where they crash-landed. Of the 11 B-29s lost over Japan, one was rammed and three were shot down by fighters.

A force of 510 Superfortresses targeted Osaka and a number of industrial targets on 26 June, and 24 Ki-44s and Ki-84s of the 246th Sentai, led by sentai commander Maj Kanshi Ishikawa, were scrambled to challenge them. Three B-29s were claimed for the loss of three pilots, including the 1st Chutai leader, Capt Sadahiko Otonari, who rammed one of the bombers and died in the collision. Otonari was credited with four B-29s destroyed and eight probables. His wingman, Sgt Minori Hara, was also killed.

On 1 July Imperial General Headquarters attempted to simplify the air defence structure by placing the 10th, 11th and 12th Air Divisions

Pilots of the 246th Sentai sit ready for action in the winter sunshine at Itami, Japan, waiting for the B-29s to arrive. Sentai commander Maj Kanshi Ishikawa is seated second from the left (*Yasuho Izawa*)

under the direct control of the Air General Army. Rather than tying all defending air units to strategic locations, they were formed into Air Defence Duty Units to provide both permanent and mobile forces that could be used to concentrate strength against major threats. The permanent forces were to be provided by four fighter regiments in the Eastern District, four regiments in the Tokai and Central Districts and one to three fighter regiments in the Western District. As part of this plan, 'Sei-Go' the 20th Fighter Group was formed from the Akeno and Hitachi Air Training Divisions in the Tokai area as part of the mobile reserve.

The permanently stationed air defence forces deployed two Ki-44 sentais within the Eastern District's 10th Air Division, namely the 23rd (20 fighters) at Imba and the 70th (29 fighters) at Kashiwa, and one Shoki sentai, the 246th (18 fighters) at Taisho, within the Central District's 11th Air Division. These were the last dedicated Ki-44 fighter units to defend Japan, and they constituted almost 31 percent of the permanently stationed force, thus demonstrating that the aircraft would continue to be an integral part of Homeland air defence to the very end.

The other permanently stationed defence fighter types were the Ki-45 'Nick' and interceptor versions of the Ki-46 (25 percent), the Ki-61 'Tony' (29 percent) and the Ki-100 – the accidental but excellent radial-engined Ki-61 hybrid (15 percent). The mobile air defence forces were equipped exclusively with the Ki-84 (66.5 percent) and the Ki-100 (33.5 percent). By this time the 47th Sentai, forming the mobile 30th Fighter Group in the Western District, together with the Ki-61/Ki-100-equipped 244th Sentai, had re-equipped entirely with the Ki-84.

Taking the air defence force as a whole, therefore, the Ki-44 still represented 18 percent of JAAF fighter air power – a tribute to the longevity and usefulness of a type that only represented nine percent of total fighter production, and whose production life had come to an end in January 1945.

After this reorganisation, the Ki-44 continued to fly and fight against the Superfortress, the Mustang and the Hellcat, its pilots believing that the final battle for the Homeland was imminent, but with no idea that a single B-29 would change things forever. The last combat casualty for the 70th Sentai occurred on 10 August over Tokyo when Capt Kanji Honda (the 1st Chutai leader) was killed in a clash with long-range Mustangs of the 15th and 506th FGs. The last major fight for the 246th Sentai came on 14 August when four Ki-44s took on a force of Mustangs, claiming one but losing Msgt Kenji Fujimoto in return.

───── CONCLUSION ─────

Both the Ki-44 'Tojo' and its Nakajima stablemate the Ki-43 'Oscar' served for almost four years in the frontline with the JAAF. The Shoki was conceived on the eve of Japan's entry into World War 2

A pilot climbs into his Ki-44 at the Akeno Flying School assisted by a mechanic. Note the retractable steps to aid cockpit access. The hinged cockpit side door is not open, and in fact the mechanic appears to be holding it shut. These doors were most often used to assist access to the cowling machine guns, together with a detachable panel in front of the windscreen (*Shigeo Hayashi via Robert C Mikesh*)

as a fast-climbing, (relatively) heavily armed fighter suitable for attacking bombers – a concept that became something of a 'side road' to the direction of actual fighter development and air fighting travel as the war progressed. Nevertheless, in the closing stages of the war the Luftwaffe resurrected this concept, and in the post-war nuclear and jet age it was again seriously pursued, with the English Electric Lightning perhaps embodying an exactly similar concept and purpose.

Ironically, it was in the originally conceived heavy fighter-versus-fighter role that the Ki-44 saw its most successful – and obscure – service, although its defence against the B-29 over the Homeland was to become iconic, if not legendary. The numbers produced, the circumstances of its deployment and the growing odds against it meant that the Ki-44 was never destined to become one of the great fighters of World War 2. But it was, and is, an interesting aircraft, significant in the development of air power generally and the Japanese fighter specifically.

For similar reasons the Shoki was never to become the mount of great aces, at least not in numbers. Those who best exploited it in the fighter-versus-fighter role had to depart from the norm of JAAF fighter pilot doctrine, and had to exploit circumstances increasingly to their disadvantage in terms of odds and what was required of them. Those who made their mark with the Ki-44 in the air defence role over Japan did so by deliberately ramming enemy bombers near the stratosphere or by stalking them at low altitude and at night and despatching them with the much dismissed 40 mm Ho-301 cannon. Neither scenario had been envisaged by the Army Staff who drew up the Shoki's original requirement specification, nor the Nakajima design team who created the fighter that met them.

The last one! The last surviving Shoki from Wright-Patterson air force base stands on display in the rain. It is identified as a 'Nakajima Tojo 2', highly polished but with a spurious emblem on the tail. Unfortunately, this last surviving Ki-44 was eventually scrapped and no intact examples of this unique aeroplane exist in the world today (*Ken Glass*)

APPENDICES

APPENDIX I

Japanese Army Aircraft Nomenclature

The somewhat complex designation of Japanese Army aeroplanes followed more than one protocol. The type number identified the year of introduction to service using the Japanese calendar and a description of the type of aircraft. Before 1939, the type number used the last two digits of the year – e.g. Type 99 for 1939 (being 2599 according to the Japanese calendar). In 1940 the type number became 100, and thereafter a single digit was used. Therefore, the Nakajima Ki-44, accepted in 1942, was the Army Type 2 single-seat fighter. The descriptive suffix was important because there was more than one Type 2 aircraft (e.g. the Kawasaki Ki-45 Toryu Type 2 two-seat fighter). The Ki-44 was unusual because it actually entered service in its pre-production form before 1942, but was only officially accepted in 1942. This type number and, usually, an abbreviated service form was the most commonly used designation during the aircraft's service, in the case of the Ki-44 the 2 Shiki Tan-za Sentoh-ki, which was abbreviated to the 2 Shiki Tan-sen.

The kitai or airframe number was a chronological listing that began in 1932, abbreviated to Ki in usage. Therefore, the Ki-44 was the 44th airframe design for the JAAF. Although little used contemporaneously, the kitai number is now often the main popular designation in use for JAAF aircraft types. Subsequent major engine or airframe changes were designated by a Roman numeral suffix to the main kitai number – e.g. Ki-44-I and Ki-44-II. A further suffix, most often used to denote armament changes, was the Imperial Japanese Army letter sequence used for equipment modifications – Ko, Otsu, Hei, Tei, Bo, Ki, Ko, Shin, Jin and Ki. Difficult to translate, these suffixes are often represented by the lower-case letters a, b, c etc. Only the first four were most commonly used.

Popular names were also assigned to the aircraft, often for propaganda or morale purposes, and the Ki-44 was called Shoki after a mythological Chinese/Japanese Taoist temple deity honoured for either destroying or frightening away demons and devils (in Chinese Zhongkui, Chung Kuei, or Chung K'uei).

The Allied reporting name or code name was a means by which airmen could quickly identify Japanese aircraft in combat reports, or for recognition purposes, without having to use the longer and potentially confusing formal Japanese designations. In general, boys' names (e.g. 'Frank') were used for fighters and girls' names (e.g. 'Sally') for other aircraft. The Ki-44 was an exception, being given the reporting name 'Tojo' after the Japanese wartime premier, Hideki Tojo. This exception probably arose because the Ki-44 was first identified in the China theatre, whereas the origin of the standard reporting code name system was in the south-west Pacific theatre.

APPENDIX II

Leading Ki-44 Aces and Ki-44 B-29 Killers

The JAAF did not officially endorse or record the concept of an 'air ace', and aircraft victories were attributed to the unit. Nevertheless, individual pilots earned reputations as aces, and individual victories have subsequently been attributed to them, with varying degrees of accuracy. During the latter part of the war the propaganda and morale value of identifying aces was exploited, but very often this centred more on the deed or deeds performed rather than the number of accumulated victories, especially where self-sacrifice was involved. This list records the leading Ki-44 aces, B-29 killers and notable pilots who flew the Shoki, but it is by no means definitive.

Name	Unit	Victories
Yasuhiko Kuroe	various	51** (4 B-29s)
Ryotaro Jobo	various	30+**
Rikio Shibata	85th Sentai	27
Naoharu Shiromoto	various	21**
Yukiyoshi Wakamatsu	85th Sentai	18+
Toshio Sakagawa	47th IFC	15**
Yoshio Yasuda*	various	10+ (6 B-29s)
Miyoshi Shimamura	85th Sentai	10
Akiyoshi Nomura	85th Sentai	10 (3 in Ki-84)
Yoshio Hirose	various	9** (1 B-29)
Yamato Takiyama	104th Sentai	9** (2 B-29s)
Kensui Kono	70th Sentai	9 B-29s
Misao Ohkubo	85th Sentai	8
Makoto Ogawa*	70th Sentai	7 B-29s
Yoshio Yoshida	70th Sentai	6 B-29s
Yoshitaro Yoshioka	9th Sentai	6
Akira Kawakita	9th Sentai	5 B-29s
Hideaki Inayama	87th Sentai	5+
Sadahiko Otonari	246th Sentai	4 B-29s + 6/8 damaged
Heikichi Yoshizawa	47th Sentai	4 B-29s
Kenji Fujimoto*	246th Sentai	3 B-29s
Tomokitsu Yamada	23rd Sentai	3 B-29s
Atsuyuki Sakato	70th Sentai	3 B-29s
Kiyoshi Otaki	70th Sentai	3 B-29s + 1 Hellcat probable

* Denotes Bukosho winners
** Not all victories claimed whilst flying the Ki-44

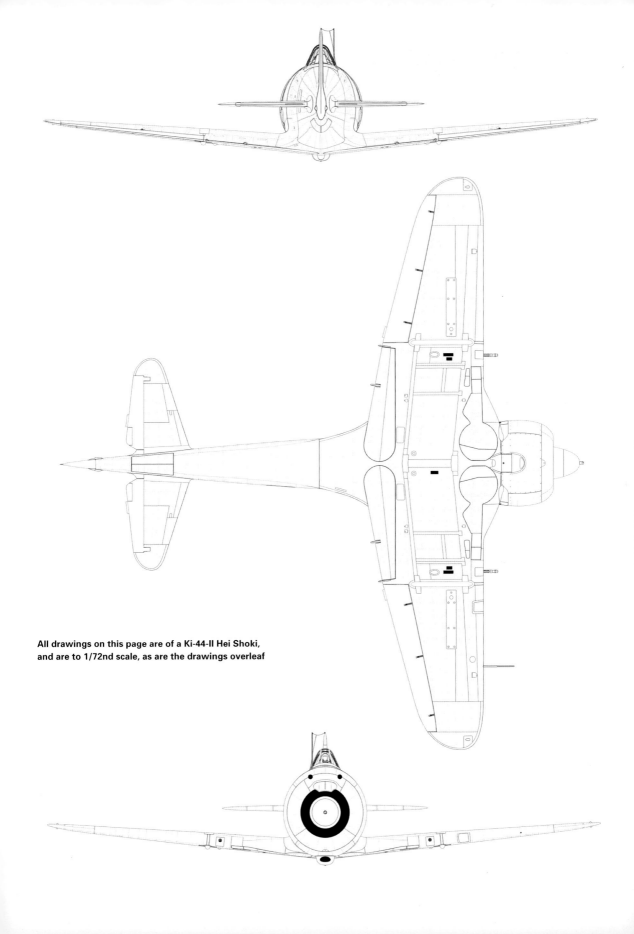

All drawings on this page are of a Ki-44-II Hei Shoki,
and are to 1/72nd scale, as are the drawings overleaf

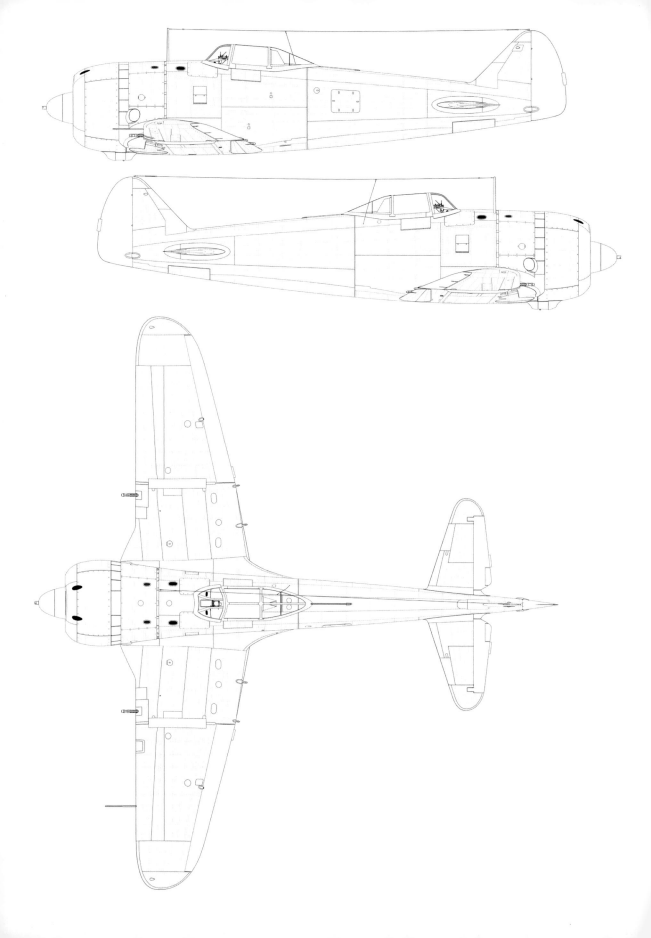

1

Pre-production Ki-44 (fifth prototype) of Maj Toshio Sakagawa, commander of the 47th Dokuritsu Hiko Chutai, Saigon, French Indochina, December 1941

Before deployment on operations, pre-production Ki-44s were painted overall in the standard JAAF hairyokushoku (grey-green) before the uppersurfaces were sprayed in an earth brown colour to give the appearance of a dense and variegated mottle. The white band around the fuselage is the senchi hiyoshiki (literally 'war front sign') to aid identification and the single diagonal white stripe on the tail signifies Sakagawa's position as both leader of the first hentai (flight) and commander of the unit.

2

Pre-production Ki-44 (eighth prototype) of Capt Yasuhiko Kuroe, 3rd Hentai Leader, 47th Dokuritsu Hiko Chutai, Kuantan, Malaya, early 1942

Capt Kuroe's aircraft is finished identically to the others in the unit except for the single red tail stripe, indicating that he was the 3rd Hentai leader (the 2nd Hentai used yellow). Beneath the cockpit is the unit's emblem, commemorating the design of the 'Yamaga-ryu' drum used to signal the attack of the 47 Ronin. Despite claiming a number of successes flying the Shoki with the Kawasemi Butai, Kuroe was a critic of the aircraft. He went on to enjoy a distinguished career flying the Ki-43 'Oscar' with the 64th Sentai in Burma and various experimental aircraft with the Army Test Centre in Japan.

3

Production series Ki-44-I of the 47th Dokuritsu Hiko Chutai, Mudon airfield, Moulmein, Burma, early 1942

The first production series Ki-44-Is were rushed to the 47th in Burma in early 1942 to make up for attritional losses. They were painted dark olive green, as the original earth brown camouflage of the pre-production aircraft was considered to be unsuitable for the jungle terrain the aircraft were operating over, and had led to some friendly fire incidents. The last two digits of the serial number '113' are painted on the tail in yellow and a large Hinomaru (sun's red disc) has been added to the fuselage sides to aid identification. The 47th's Ki-44s were amongst the first JAAF fighters to carry the marking in this position.

4

Ki-44-I of the 33rd Sentai, Canton, China, early 1943

This aircraft is a partially speculative representation of the first Ki-44-Is issued to the 33rd Sentai in China and formed into a special flight under the command of sentai CO, Maj Akira Watanabe. The unusual camouflage and markings are reconstructed from a detailed intelligence report and partial photographs. Intended as 'sky camouflage', the grey colours imitated Luftwaffe practice. Although the 33rd pioneered the deployment of the Ki-44 in China, it was predominantly an 'Oscar' unit, and after leaving China in the autumn of 1943 it did not continue to use the new fighter.

5

Ki-44-II Ko of Capt Yukiyoshi Wakamatsu, 2nd Chutai leader, 85th Sentai, Hankow, China, summer 1943

Capt Wakamatsu was to become one of the most successful combat leaders and exponents of the Ki-44 in China, being dubbed the 'Red Nose Ace' by friend and foe alike. This aircraft attributed to him displays one of the many colourful camouflage schemes applied by the unit, and it is believed to be accurately depicted here for the first time. The olive green was sprayed directly over the natural metal of the airframe in a horizontal sweeping motion and then blotches and squiggles of brown ('tea colour') were applied over the green. The red tail insignia is in abbreviated form and the red Hinomaru and fuselage band, indicating a chutai leader, show evidence of being masked off when the camouflage was applied. The serial number of the aircraft also appears on a masked off panel of natural metal in the centre of this band.

6

Ki-44-II Ko of Capt Yukiyoshi Wakamatsu, 2nd Chutai Leader, 85th Sentai, Tien Ho airfield, Canton, China, summer 1943

This aircraft, also flown by Capt Wakamatsu, displays an unusual variation of the 85th Sentai insignia and is unpainted, apart from the 2nd Chutai leader's fuselage band and red spinner. The metal surface has oxidised in the south China climate of strong sun and high humidity, giving it an almost dull grey appearance. The fabric control surfaces – ailerons, elevators and rudder – are painted in the standard hairyokushoku grey-green colour. Capt Wakamatsu led two flights of free-ranging Ki-44s over central and south-west China during 1943-44.

7

Ki-44-II Hei of Capt Yukiyoshi Wakamatsu, 2nd Chutai Leader, 85th Sentai, Canton, China, summer 1944

Some of the 85th's Ki-44s were painted in an overall blue-grey colour before the green and brown camouflage was applied (and some were briefly flown in the blue-grey before being camouflaged). This is one example that displays the full sentai insignia of a half-arrow in the 2nd Chutai's red colour, with a white Kanji character for 'Waka' identifying the pilot. The red fuselage band identifies Wakamatsu as the 2nd Chutai leader. The spinner is painted red, and it is possible that the forward cowling ring on this aircraft was also the same colour. Although Wakamatsu (and the 85th) began flying the Ki-84 Hayate in the late autumn of 1944, the new type's unreliability prompted him to retain a Ki-44 for his own use. By the end of the war the 85th was flying a mix of both types.

8

Ki-44-II Ko of 2nd Chutai, 85th Sentai, Hankow, China, summer 1943

This aircraft represents the wingmen who flew in Capt Wakamatsu's 2nd Chutai. The character 'Ha' on the tail probably represents the first syllable of the pilot's surname.

The aircraft is painted in an unusual olive green 'mesh' camouflage depicted here over the natural metal of the airframe. However, some sources interpret this aircraft as having a sandy brown colour under the green. Camouflage was driven by the exigencies of the air campaign and was not consistent or permanent. Aircraft initially flown unpainted might subsequently be camouflaged, dependent upon how long they lasted and the tempo of air operations.

9

Ki-44-II Ko of Capt Akira Horaguchi, 1st Chutai Leader, 85th Sentai, Wuchang, China, summer 1943

Some of the 1st Chutai's Ki-44s had a thin coat of black paint applied over their brown and green camouflage. The reason for this is unknown, but these aircraft were frequently described by US pilots as belonging to the 'Black Dragon' squadron, and were identified as IJNAF Zero-sens. The white half-arrow on the tail signifies the 1st Chutai and the white fuselage band Capt Horaguchi's status as 1st Chutai leader. The forward cowling ring is unpainted, possibly in preparation for being painted white. Ki-44s painted black overall, and with white cowling bands, were reported in encounters over south China during the autumn and winter of 1943-44. Capt Horaguchi was shot down and killed over Changteh on 4 December 1943 by P-40s of the 74th FS/23rd FG.

10

Ki-44-II Hei of the 50th Sentai, Meiktila, Burma, 1944

The 50th Sentai was a predominantly Ki-43 'Oscar'-equipped unit, but like its Burma companions the 64th Sentai, it used a small number of Ki-44s over central Burma and during the Imphal offensive. This fighter's unusual hard-edged blotch camouflage over the natural metal is reconstructed from a photograph of an abandoned aircraft, but the colour of the unit's distinctive lightning bolt is speculative. In some references it is reported to be in the 2nd Chutai's yellow colour, but this remained unconfirmed. These Ki-44s were drawn from the Field Air Supply Depot at Singapore.

11

Ki-44-II Ko of Lt Shiro Suzuki, 4th Chutai, 64th Sentai, Rangoon, Burma, late 1943

The famous 'Oscar'-equipped 64th Sentai spent the whole war fighting over Burma, and formed a 4th Chutai of Ki-44 aircraft for air defence duties over Rangoon in response to increasing Allied bomber raids. The unit's distinctive tail arrow insignia is shown here in green, the recognised 4th Chutai colour, but this is speculative, and it might well have been cobalt blue for the Sentai HQ staff flight (Sentai Hombu) or 3rd Chutai yellow. Lt Suzuki was killed in combat fighting P-51 Mustangs over Rangoon on 27 November 1943.

12

Ki-44-II Otsu of the 87th Sentai, Meiktila, Burma, May 1944

This aircraft is representative of the 40 mm cannon-armed Otsu versions of the Ki-44 flown into Burma by the 87th Sentai during May 1944. The standard armament configuration for the Otsu variant was 12.7 mm cowling weapons and no wing armament, with the 40 mm Ho-301 fitted as special equipment. The camouflage scheme consists of an olive green mottle painted directly over the natural metal airframe.

The mottle was applied in various patterns that were not consistent throughout the unit. The profile is based on film footage of the 87th in Burma and Allied intelligence reports describing abandoned aircraft at Meiktila.

13

Ki-44-II Hei of Lt Hideaki Inayama, 87th Sentai, Gloembang, Sumatra, January 1945

Lt Inayama's distinctive black-grey, thinly painted Shoki carries the sentai emblem of the billowing 'bag of wind' carried by the Shinto God of the Wind, Fûjin. It is usually depicted in red for the 2nd Chutai, but Inayama himself described his flight markings as being applied in blue paint. The blue fuselage band indicates Inayama's 1st Shotai leader status and the wing tips might also have been painted blue. By this time the unit had re-organised from chutai to hikotai composition, and the precise presentation of command markings is unknown. The depiction is partly speculative, being based on descriptions of the aircraft from veterans of the 87th.

14

Ki-44-II Ko of Sgt Tadashi Kikukawa, 85th Sentai, Canton, China, late 1943

This aircraft has often been attributed to the 22nd Sentai because of the Kikusui emblem on the tail, but at the time a photograph of this Ki-44 appeared in a commemorative book published by the Japanese newspaper *Mainichi* in November 1943, the 22nd had not even been established. The emblem is now believed to be just a personal motif representing the pilot's name (Kiku = chrysanthemum, and Kawa = river) with the aircraft belonging to the 85th Sentai. This emblem might have been applied purely for the purpose of the press release. Sgt Kikukawa was killed in action over Suichuan, in China, on 12 February 1944.

15

Ki-44-II Otsu of the 1st Chutai, 23rd Sentai, Imba, Japan, 1945

Representative of the Ki-44 aircraft flown by this Home Defence unit in its battles against the B-29, this fighter's tail emblem is a simple graphic representation of the numbers '2' and '3'. By the time the 23rd was formed in October 1944 from the Ohta Air Training Unit of the Hitachi Training Air Division, Ki-44s were being painted at the factory in an olive brown colour. However, this aircraft appears to be an earlier production model camouflaged in dark green. One of the most notable pilots of the 23rd Sentai was Sgt Tomokitsu Yamada, who claimed four B-29s destroyed. This aircraft has had the armament removed and cowling apertures faired over for air-to-air ramming attacks.

16

Ki-44-II Otsu of the 3rd Chutai, 70th Sentai, Anshan, Manchuria, August 1944

This glossy dark green-painted Ki-44 was unusual for the 70th Sentai, as the majority of their aircraft remained in natural metal finish. Another notable feature is the absence of wing armament – standard configuration for the Otsu. Although the white 'bandages' to the Hinomaru were intended only for Home Defence recognition purposes, the rapid transfer of this unit from Japan to Manchuria in August 1944 meant they were still carried by aircraft flying from Anshan.

17

Ki-44-II Hei of the Sentai Hombu, 29th Sentai, Clark Field, the Philippines, November 1944

The sweeping 'arrow wave' symbol of the 29th Sentai was, for many years, assumed to have been worn only by the unit's Ki-84s in Formosa, until a photograph revealed the emblem on a Ki-44 in the Philippines. The 29th, a former reconnaissance unit hastily converted to fighters, was sent to Clark Field in November 1944 following the Leyte landings, and it suffered badly in the ill-fated defence of the islands prior to being withdrawn to Formosa in January 1945. The unit lost 15 pilots (including two chutai leaders) in just three engagements in November and December 1944.

18

Ki-44-II Hei of the 29th Sentai, Hsiaochiang, Formosa, August 1944

Depicted here shortly before its temporary deployment to Wuchang, in China, in August 1944 to reinforce JAAF units in-theatre, this Ki-44 displays a dramatic horned skull marking on the tail that was possibly a personal emblem. The unit was to enjoy no better fortune in China than it had done in the Philippines, with few engagements but several losses. The profile of this aircraft has been partly reconstructed from an incomplete photograph, and elements of the tail marking are therefore speculative.

19

Ki-44-II Hei 'Asakaze' of the 2nd Chutai, 104th Sentai, Mukden, Manchuria, autumn 1944

Prior to re-equipment with the Ki-84 'Frank' fighter, the 104th briefly flew Ki-44s from bases in Manchuria on air defence duties, challenging the first B-29 raids against Anshan. Each aircraft was given a name, in this case 'Asakaze' ('Morning Breeze'), the Shoki depicted here being representative of the Ki-44s that saw action against the B-29s in China. Other examples known to have served with the 104th at this time were 'Kitakaze' (Northern Wind) and 'Kochikaze' (Eastern Wind). Each chutai marked the propeller spinners, wing tips and fin tips of their Ki-44s in their assigned colours, with the 2nd using yellow, as seen here – the 1st Chutai used red and the 3rd Chutai blue. The practice of naming aircraft was continued with the Ki-84, but the dramatic emblem of a large dagger or sword on the tail was discontinued with the new fighter.

20

Ki-44-I of the 47th Dokuritsu Hiko Chutai, Kashiwa, Japan, late 1942

After returning to Japan the 47th was issued with Ki-44 fighters in natural metal (unpainted) finish. Prior to adopting a new unit emblem representing a stylised '4' and '7', the squadron applied large two-digit numbers to the painted tail fin which probably represented the last two digits of each aircraft's serial number – in this case 134, manufactured during August 1942. Early versions of the wing leading edge IFF stripes were painted in red rather than yellow, but the aircraft already displays the 'bandages' behind the fuselage Hinomaru, identifying its Home Defence role. The Ki-44-I variant can be identified by the absence of an oil cooler under the cowling, the aircraft having an annular oil cooler located within the cowling instead.

21

Ki-44-II Hei of Capt Teiichi Hitano, 3rd Chutai/Hikotai and 'Sakura' Leader, 47th Sentai, Narimasu, Japan, early 1944

By the time the 47th had worked up to full sentai status the unit's tail emblem comprised a second version of a stylistic representation of the numbers '4' and '7', as shown here. Each chutai was distinguished by displaying this emblem in different colours, with a yellow emblem outlined in red for the 3rd Chutai. When the 47th adopted a hikotai rather than chutai organisation from January 1944, the three sub-units were named 'Asahi', 'Fuji' and 'Sakura' respectively. The chutai/hikotai leader's aircraft had a broad fuselage band and fin tip painted in the command colour of cobalt blue. The tail number is depicted here as '80' as seen in a photograph of the aircraft, but it has often been reported as '66'.

22

Ki-44-II Otsu of MSgt Isamu Sakamoto of Shinten Seikutai, 47th Sentai, Narimasu, Japan, late 1944

The aircraft of the 47th's air-to-air ramming flights were gaudily painted, at first identified by red tails and a large, winged 'Yamaga-ryu' drum emblem. This aircraft has had its cowling armament removed and gun apertures faired over. MSgt Sakamoto deliberately rammed a B-29 over Musashi on 27 January 1945 and survived the collision. He was awarded the Bukosho 2nd Class for this feat.

23

Ki-44-II Otsu of Capt Jun Shimizu, 1st Chutai, 47th Sentai, Narimasu, Japan, 1944

This 40 mm cannon-armed Ki-44 was possibly an aircraft flown by the 1st Chutai leader, Capt Jun Shimizu, and it was painted to identify it as a supporting aircraft for the ramming flights. Ki-44 serial number 1435 was manufactured in September 1943. Where possible, pairs of fighters coordinated gunnery and ramming attacks, and it required strong nerves to fly close enough to a B-29 for the slow-firing 40 mm cannon to be effective. The red tail emblem identifies the chutai to which the Ki-44 was assigned, but the marking itself is plain, without the usual black outline. The cobalt blue band signifies the pilot's command or staff status. The unusual red IFF strips on the wings are based on the careful study of contemporary photographs.

24

Ki-44-II Hei of Capt Yazuro Mazaki, 2nd Chutai, 47th Sentai, Narimasu, Japan, late 1944

This Ki-44 was one of the aircraft flown by Capt Mazaki, and it is equipped with wing racks for dropping Ta-dan aerial bombs in the path of B-29 formations. At the end of November 1944 Capt Mazaki switched to the Ki-84 Hayate at the Army Test Centre, and thereafter he helped other 47th pilots transition onto the new fighter. In early December 1944 he was transferred to the Hitachi Training Air Division as an instructor. The 47th became the first permanent air defence unit to transition to the Ki-84 after its long spell with the Ki-44.

25

Ki-44-II Hei of the 246th Sentai, Clark Field, the Philippines, late 1944

This aircraft is representative of the hastily camouflaged Ki-44s sent to the Philippines in response to the American landings on

Leyte. The colours used were typically 'karekusa iro' (dried grass) and olive green sprayed over the natural metal of the airframe. The spinner spiral is unusual but not unique for JAAF aircraft. The sentai emblem represented a diving swallow set against the sun's red disk, but was humorously referred to as 'umeboshi' (a pickled red plum), the black swallow being likened to chopsticks laid on the dish.

26
Ki-44-II Hei of the 246th Sentai, Taisho, Japan, winter 1944-45
After their return from disastrous experiences in the Philippines, some aircraft of the unit displayed a simple red horizontal band on the tail, representing a loyal and sincere state of mind. This aircraft retains the traditional emblem, and has three fuselage stripes perhaps as chutai or flight command markings. The full panoply of Home Defence 'bandages' as an aid to recognition are worn behind the wing and fuselage Hinomaru. The 246th remained active in the Nagoya, Osaka and Kobe areas, flying Ki-44 air defence sorties over Tokyo until the end of the war, specialising in both the night interception and air-to-air bombing roles.

27
Ki-44-II Hei of Capt Yoshio Yoshida, 70th Sentai, Kashiwa, Japan, 1945
Bukosho winner Capt Yoshida was one of the celebrated B-29 hunters of the 70th Sentai but, dramatic depictions to the contrary, he scored most of his bomber kills at night using a 40 mm cannon-armed Otsu version of the Ki-44. His aircraft is elaborately marked and dated for each of his B-29 victories, possibly for morale or even propaganda purposes, and it displays the large number '11'. The tail emblem, usually shown as yellow, is depicted here in red in accordance with recent research in Japan that provides credible evidence for that colour.

28
Ki-44-II Hei of WO Makoto Ogawa, 70th Sentai, Kashiwa, Japan, 1945
WO Ogawa was another Bukosho-winning B-29 ace of the 70th, finishing the war with seven claims for big bombers destroyed, as well as two P-51s. His unpainted Ki-44 was also elaborately marked with eagles for each victory, as well as the large number '2'. Six eagles are usually depicted in illustrations of this aircraft. The position of the sixth eagle is uncertain but was unlikely to have been painted over the white Homeland Defence band. Several previous illustrations, in order to include the sixth eagle without encroaching on the white band, have altered its width and moved the Hinomaru rearwards. Ogawa also preferred to hunt at night, making risky attacks by approaching the B-29 formations from head-on and below. On being awarded the Bukosho, he was promoted to second lieutenant. The Hei variant of the Ki-44 can be identified by the larger access panel on the side of the nose, which covered the magazine for the 12.7 mm cowling weapons, and by the reflector type gunsight.

29
Ki-44-II Hei of the 3rd Chutai, 9th Sentai, Anking, China 1944
Representative of the aircraft flown by 9th Sentai ace Yoshitaro Yoshioka, this heavily weathered example displays the unit's tail emblem, which was said to simply represent

the number '9' (kyu). Some references, however, describe it as a representation of the weapon carried by the historical warrior Kiyomasa Kato and the character 'na' for the name of the sentai commander, Lt Col Seisaku Namba. By the end of the war the 9th was flying a mixed complement of Ki-44s and Ki-84s. Lt Yoshioka had the distinction of making two deadstick landings in the Ki-44, although on the second occasion he was seriously injured. He eventually returned to the unit, and was instrumental in maintaining morale and leadership in the face of increasing adversity. After the war Yoshioka remained in China to train local pilots to fly the Ki-84, and he subsequently served in the Japan Self-Defence Army, rising to the rank of lieutenant colonel.

30
Ki-44-I of the Akeno Army Flying School, Japan, 1943
This early production Ki-44-II of the Akeno Army Flying School was adorned with spurious RAF markings and flown by the future 68th Sentai ace Lt Hiroshi Sekiguchi for the making of the feature film Kato Hayabusa Sentōtai during 1943, a Toho Co Ltd movie about the 64th Sentai commander Maj Tateo Kato. Ironically, a handful of identically marked Ki-44s were used to play the part of RAF Brewster Buffalo fighters in distant shots showing the interception of Ki-21 bombers. The aircraft retains the distinctive symbol of the Akeno School on its rudder, however. Akeno operated at least two hikotai of Ki-44s for advanced fighter pilot training. Lt Sekiguchi achieved seven aerial victories from 1937 to 1945, serving in the 5th Rentai, 64th and 68th Sentais over New Guinea and 105th Sentai over Japan.

31
Ki-44-II Hei of Capt Ryotaro Jobo, 1st Field Reserve Air Unit, Singapore, 1944
Capt Jobo flew Ki-44s with the fighter squadron of this unit against the first B-29 attacks on Singapore, specialising in the operational testing of air-to-air rocket weapons. Capt Jobo was a Nomonhan veteran with 18 Soviet fighters to his credit, and he eventually claimed more than 30 aerial victories. A master swordsman, he survived the war. Inspired by a rare photograph, this aircraft is painted in the late-war factory scheme of olive brown, with a simple unit emblem and number on the tail and the distinguishing markings of a white-painted fin leading edge (and possibly spinner). The emblem is said to represent the katakana character 'Ho' for Hoju (from the unit designation 1st Yasen Hójú Hikótai) in the form of a stylised bird or aeroplane over an upturned crescent. This group flew examples of most JAAF types organised into fighter, light bomber, medium bomber and reconnaissance squadrons. In addition to providing training for replacement pilots scheduled to serve in squadrons assigned to the 3rd and 4th Air Armies, the 1st Field Reserve Air Unit conducted dissimilar combat training using captured aircraft and developed air tactics and weapons.

32
Ki-44-II Hei of Maj Yoshio Hirose, 1st Hikotai of Hitachi TAD, Mito, Japan, December 1944
Typical of the aircraft that equipped the Secondary Provisional Units (Tō Ni Go Butai) formed within the Training Air Divisions to augment interception capability against the B-29 threat, this Ki-44 was flown by Maj Yoshio Hirose of the Hitachi Training

Air Division (Hitachi Kyodo Hikoshidan). The red lightning bolt was Maj Hirose's personal marking. Hirose had a distinguished career in the JAAF, claiming victories from 1937 onwards and serving with distinction in the 64th Sentai over Burma. His dedicated service was recognised by a presentation to the Emperor following his posting to Hitachi. He was killed on 22 December 1944 when he deliberately rammed a B-29.

BIBLIOGRAPHY

Birdsall, Steve, *Saga of the Superfortress*, Sidgwick & Jackson, London, 1981

Chennault, Claire C, *Way of a Fighter*, Thorvardson & Sons, Tucson, 1991

Ferkl, Martin, *Nakajima Ki-44 Shoki*, Revi Publications, Ostrava-Paruba, Czech Republic, 2009

Hata, Ikuhiko, Izawa, Yasuho and Shores, Christopher, *Japanese Army Air Force Fighter Units And Their Aces 1931-1945*, Grub Street, London, 2002

Japan Defence Agency, *Army Air Operations in Southeast Asia*, Asagumo Shimbunsha, Tokyo, 1970

Japan Defence Agency, *Army Air Operations in China*, Asagumo Shimbunsha, Tokyo, 1974

Kanzaki, Col Kiyoshi and Others, *Homeland Air Defense Operations Record,* Japanese Monographs Nos 157-159, HQ USAFFE and 8th Army, Tokyo, 1952

Kissick Jr, Luther C, *Guerilla One,* Sunflower University Press, Yuma, 1983

Kuroe, Yasuhiko, *Aa Hayabusa Sentotai*, Kojinsha, Tokyo, 1969

Mann, Robert A, *The B-29 Superfortress*, McFarland and Company, Inc., Jefferson, North Carolina, 2004

Molesworth, Carl and Moseley, Steve, *Wing to Wing – Air Combat in China 1943-45*, Orion Books, New York, 1990

Molesworth, Carl, *Sharks Over China – 23rd FG in World War 2*, Brassey's, Washington, 1994

Nohara, Shigeru, *Nakajima Ki-44 Shoki*, Model Art, Tokyo, 2009

Sakaida, Henry, *Osprey Aircraft of the Aces 13 - Japanese Army Air Force Aces 1937-45*, Osprey, Botley, Oxford, England 1997

Shiba, Maj Takira and Others, *Air Defense of the Homeland,* Japanese Monograph No 23, HQ USAFFE and 8th Army, Tokyo, 1956

Shiba, Maj Takira and Others, *Air Operations in the China Area 1937-1945*, Japanese Monograph No 76, HQ USAFFE and 8th Army, Tokyo, 1956

Takaki, Koji and Sakaida, Henry, *Osprey Aviation Elite Units 6 - B-29 Hunters of the JAAF*, Osprey, Botley, Oxford, England, 2001

Tanaka, Masa, *Burma Air Operations Record Jan 1942 – Aug 1945*, Japanese Monograph No 64, HQ USAFFE and 8th Army, Tokyo, 1946

Umemoto, Hiroshi, *Air Combat Over China of Ki-44 and Ki-84 in 1943-45, 9th & 85th Sentais*, Dainippon Kaiga, Japan, 2008

Watanabe, Yohji, *Pictorial History of Air War Over Japan – Japanese Army Air Force*, Hara-Shobo Co. Ltd., Tokyo, 1980

INDEX